A chance encounter at a sea-front amusement arcade. An unrequited love. A funeral. All the elements of an obsessive passion, but distorted to the point of delirium through pin-ups, movies and gossip columns.

*Waiting for Bardot* is not a biography of Brigitte Bardot but a mythography, an elegy for an icon. Sexual messiah and existential heroine, feminist and fantasy, the archetypal woman who gave up men for beasts: BB has been the mirror of our desires and anxieties.

*Waiting for Bardot* is, above all, a true romance, the record of a lopsided love-affair, framed by celluloid. In the utopian summer of 1968 the author and his best friend and arch-rival, Griffo, set out for St Tropez to consummate their teenage lust. A quarter of a century later they end up on an empty beach of black sand in Ireland – still waiting for Bardot. But out of the ashes of experience the dream is born again.

Andy Martin first fell under the spell of Brigitte Bardot at the age of 8½. He returned from St Tropez to write *The Knowledge of Ignorance* and *Walking on Water*. He now teaches French at Cambridge.

# Waiting for Bardot

ANDY MARTIN

*faber and faber*

LONDON · BOSTON

First published in 1996
by Faber and Faber Limited
3 Queen Square London WC1N 3AU

Photoset by Parker Typesetting Service, Leicester
Printed in England by Clays Ltd, St Ives plc

© Andy Martin, 1996
Copyright for the photographs in the plate section is held by the following:
1 and 7a: The Kobal Collection
2: The Ronald Grant Archive
3, 5, 6a and 6b: Hulton Getty Picture Collection Ltd
4: Reveille, 31 October 1957, by permission of the Syndics of
Cambridge University Library
6c: The Steve Griffen Collection
6d: Courtesy of BFI Stills, Posters and Designs
7b: John Hilleson Agency Ltd

Andy Martin is hereby identified as author of this
work in accordance with Section 77 of the Copyright,
Designs and Patents Act 1988

A CIP record for this book
is available from the British Library

ISBN 0-571-17871-5

2 4 6 8 10 9 7 5 3 1

# Contents

For Griffo
who asked 'Where's me Bloody Book then ya Bold Bollox?'

If we wish to understand what BB represents, it is useless to make the acquaintance of the young woman named Brigitte Bardot.

Simone de Beauvoir, *Brigitte Bardot and the Lolita Syndrome*

## PART ONE

# Hate

There lived a singer in France of old
By the tideless dolorous midland sea.
In a land of sand and ruin and gold
There shone one woman, and none but she.
Swinburne, 'The Triumph of Time'

# 1

# September 1966

Come outside, come outside,
there's a luvverly moon out there.
Mike Sarne, 'Come Outside'

In the beginning was the Word and the Word became flesh some time in the second week of September 1966, when BB had carnal knowledge of Mike Sarne. Technically she was married to Gunther Sachs at the time. 'Count' Gunther Fritz Sachs von Opel: multi-millionaire German playboy, scion of the motor-car dynasty and European bobsleigh champion of 1958, a crack shot with both gun and club. One of the gods. Up there with Sean Connery and Roger Vadim, the creator himself. But Sarne was virtually one of us, a low-born Londoner. Brigitte Bardot had miraculously fallen to earth.

Mike Sarne had first thrust himself upon our attention as far back as the summer of 1962 when he brought out a single which went to No. 1 and tragically echoed our own futile and fumbling efforts to score with girls. Most of the song consisted of Sarne trying to chat up (in caricature Cockney) a *little doll* with laughable lines about the moon and how lovely it was and wouldn't she like to see it. If you just want to go on *dancing*, he rhymes, there won't be any time left for *romancing*. Obviously the poor sod doesn't stand a chance. And then, right at the end of the record, she – won over or worn out by his verbals? – finally caves in.

And now, it seemed, he had lured Bardot outside too. While Wendy Richards, his hit-parade paramour, was scripted to marry Arthur in *EastEnders* and breed children destined for single-parenthood or HIV, Sarne would go on more gloriously to direct the catastrophic screen version of Gore Vidal's *Myra Breck-*

3

*inridge* (starring Raquel Welch) in 1970. Whether he succeeded in notching up another sex-symbol is, so far as I know, unrecorded, and beside the point. For there is no doubt that Sarne's apogee, his high noon, the climax of his career, was Bardot and September 1966.

Naturally, our reaction was complex and ambivalent. 'That fuckin' weedy rat pulling BB!?' spluttered Griffo, 'Not that poncey little git!' But there was a degree of hot-headed subjectivity mixed up in this preliminary judgement. This coupling, this collision, seemed to us at first sight a bizarre freak of nature, an aberration in the order of things, a joke. In the light of a later, more measured assessment, it is possible to lay out the facts, such as we came to know them, coolly and calmly, and divine the subcutaneous structure of history in all its inevitability.

BB was in Scotland to shoot an Anglo-French production, *Two Weeks in September* (or *A coeur joie* as it is obscurely known in French): every scene had to be filmed twice over, once in French and once in English. She had married Sachs not two months before, in July, after a typical multi-millionaire playboy whirlwind wooing involving gross-loads of roses, private jets, Bastille Day, at least one Kennedy, Danny Kaye and a judge in Las Vegas. But two months was a long time in sixties sexual politics: two weeks was a long time. After a honeymoon in Tahiti, swimming in coral lagoons and drinking milk straight from the coconut, and then a spell in Acapulco to recover, how could BB not be bored?

When she flew in to Heathrow on 3 September in a green and yellow tartan mini-skirt, greeted by the ritual chant of *Bri-gitte! Bri-gitte!*, she flew in alone (not counting one PR man, her co-star, two or three personal photographers and one man whose job it was to carry her vanity bag). She was happy to be returning to work. 'It is good to have a change,' she told reporters. 'Honeymoon, work, honeymoon, work.' The implication was clear: once the film was over she would feel a compulsive need for another wedding, another husband. Unless she was planning to change lovers between takes.

Perhaps Sachs intuited as much while doing some shooting of his own in the Black Forest because he hastened to Scotland to play a few rounds of golf, à la Connery. But, immune as his bride

4

was to the joys of a full bag of clubs and a Scottish sand-trap, this only served as a provocation. Five minutes after he'd flown off again she revealed exclusively to hordes of journalists that she was already feeling lonely: 'I am living on memories ... Unfortunately no one can live on memories.'

Bardot's part would not have stretched her acting ability. The film was an obvious allegory of her marriage to Sachs, complete with a symbolically overloaded scene in which a wedding-dress is torn from her throbbing body. Suffocated by her possessive publisher-lover, Cécile takes advantage of a modelling assignment in London to embark on a series of liaisons. First comes the photographer (Sarne). This was standard for the period, when any male equipped with a functioning camera was ipso facto irresistible. Next in line is a geologist, who, pursuing her from Paris, mines a deep vein of passion against the background of a ruined castle in the Scottish highlands. The fortnight leaves us dangling, however, with BB at the end, like a gourmet sizing up the menu, hesitating as to which lover to choose.

On celluloid, as on vinyl, Sarne is cocky and self-assured, and why wouldn't he be, what with having his way with any woman he waves his lens at? But he is out-manoeuvred by the French geologist (Laurent Terzieff, whom Bardot had shoe-horned into the part). Off the set it was another story. Against all the odds – on paper, no more than an also-ran alongside the likes of Terzieff, Sachs and Bob Zagury (an ex-lover who had followed her from St Tropez) – Sarne seduced a myth.

Despite our infinite dismissiveness for the man himself, we nevertheless sensed even then that he had stumbled upon a fundamental truth. He – we – could not compete with the Gunther Sachses of this world, with their Lear jets and flunkies. The point was not to compete, not even to seek out the object of desire. You had to wait and be ready. And then the miracle would happen and she would come to you. You could not actively *pull* Bardot, but only be pulled, sucked in, swept up in the storm.

Sarne had to be vetted by BB before the picture started. She was shown a mugshot in Paris and stamped him with her seal of approval. Bardot, like a lawyer weeding out potentially antipathetic jurors, had right of veto over co-stars. When Roger Vadim unveiled a picture of Jean-Louis Trintignant, then a young unknown he wanted to play her husband in *Et Dieu créa la femme*, she turned him down flat. 'Why don't you find me a handsome boy?' she objected. 'Why this boy? He is so odd-looking!' But, under pressure from Vadim, she relented, and kept on relenting, almost as if to punish her director-husband.

She had a habit of falling for co-stars. It was method acting taken to its biological conclusion. Don't pretend to have sex: *have* sex; don't act insatiable: *be* insatiable. It was as if Bardot had chosen, at some point, to draw no distinction between on- and off-screen, the simulacrum and the real. The studio and the bedroom were all one to her.

I would have liked to have seen that shot of Sarne. Was there some special trick of the light, some angle, that particularly beguiled her? Sarne wasn't ugly, but he was no Connery, not even – to our eyes – a Trintignant, who could pass for a French James Dean. No, he was an ordinary sort of bloke, with straight rather thinning hair, hollow cheeks, eyes, nose, mouth all so-so. Rex Reed once described him as resembling a wolf with rabies. But that detail only underscored the unbelievable truth: she, Brigitte Bardot, the ultimate woman in the universe, fell (however fleetingly) for Mike Sarne, who lived to the west of London, just as we symmetrically lived to the east.

Once she had okayed the photograph, everything was permitted. Everything was just about compulsory, axiomatic. BB, barely waiting for Sachs to catch the plane, took this supposed no-hoper to her boudoir. Sarne's detractors say that he was too self-absorbed, too much the narcissist to have any success with women. But, as Peter Evans in *Bardot: The Eternal Goddess*, shrewdly observes, 'He must have been doing something right.'

'Studied indifference' is the canonical theory about Sarne's strategy: the Joe Cool act. But Sir Alf Ramsey had a hand in it too. Bobby Moore and his boys winning the World Cup at the end of July 1966, beating West Germany in the final at Wembley, 4–2 after extra-time, was what really set Sarne up. Sarne vs Sachs in September was a replay of England vs West Germany, just as the match itself had been a replay of the Second World War. History repeats itself, the first time round as tragedy, the second as football and the third as sex. There was a direct genealogy between, at one end of the pitch, Hitler, Franz Beckenbauer and Sachs, and, at the other end, Churchill, Geoff Hurst and Sarne. The outcome of the match was a foregone conclusion. It was a walkover.

Factor in to this initial disposition of forces geographical and metereological phenomena. *Two Weeks in September* required its heroine to spend two weeks in inadequate clothing on a blasted beach in East Lothian in September, a few degrees south of the Arctic Circle, where several portable generators had had to be trucked in, one exclusively for her personal hair-dryer. The local fire brigade stood ready, with their single but powerful engine, to hose BB and her partners down with foam should things get too hot – or too dry. Not only were they not needed, given the frequency of natural fire-extinguishing rain, but BB had to resort to putting on a chunky cardigan off-camera. But she didn't like cardigans. Cardigans were unknown on the kind of beaches she was used to. So she took to wrapping Sarne around her instead.

Sublimely contemptuous of director Serge Bourguignon, Bardot and Sarne *went underground* or were *in limbo*, after which BB began giving interviews openly critical of her husband and musing that 'love is the greatest illusion'. They shacked up together in Paris when the production shifted back to the Billancourt Studios. So far so normal. But then something happened that exploded all preconceptions and marked a major paradigm-shift in our conception of BB. It transpired that Sarne had spirited her off to his Chiswick flat for a weekend and, still more incredibly, escorted her down Chiswick High Street.

Then she chucked him.

But this was incidental, BB's characteristic signature, her standard punctuation, a footnote to the substantive history. The actual duration of the affair was of academic interest only. The legend had walked among the pages of the *A–Z*. That was the crux. It was obvious that she wasn't going to stick it out and take up residence: BB and W4 are separate worlds. Like an alien being whose UFO had crash-landed, she couldn't breathe the atmosphere in Chiswick. If Jesus Christ had been reported turning water to wine in Romford market-place we couldn't have been more amazed. If not for the pictures, we would never have believed it. BB had made the supreme sacrifice, to save us.

It took us a while to attain this level of wisdom. Our first thoughts were of violation, blasphemy, sacrilege. 'That little prick Sarne, pronging BB!' moaned Griffo. 'That piece o' piss!' But when Sachs raged and fumed and spat in one of his Bavarian castles, it was clear that the impossible had indeed occurred. When logic possessed us once more, it was with the irrefragible force of a syllogism that the understanding came upon us that we too were contenders: we too were in line for that crowning moment of ecstasy – a spell in bed with Brigitte Bardot.

And as soon as it became possible it also became necessary and – such was the optimism of the times – inevitable. In the second half of the sixties, in the thick of the Apollo space programme, with the Jules Rimez trophy standing on our mantlepiece, insane crackpot fantasies made perfect sense. BB embodied for us, as for the massed manhood of the western world, the sexual Shangri-la of the future. Brigitte Bardot was as remote as Ruritania, but John Glenn, Neil Armstrong, Griffo and I, we had the hardware, we had the know-how, we had the desire, we could shoot at the moon and expect to score before the decade was out, as surely as if we were Geoff Hurst and BB were BeckenBauer.

# 2

## Summer 1961

Dip-de-dip-dip-dip, bum-ba-ba-bum, ba-bum-ba-bum-
bum, bum-ba-bum-bum, dang-a-dang-dang, ding-a-
dong-ding.

The Marcels, 'Blue Moon'

My romance with BB had started long before, the summer I
foresaw that Marilyn Monroe would die a premature death.

I remember the beginning of that year well: the front cover of
*The Beano* showed that 1961 read the same upside down as
right-way-up. Lonnie Donegan was still skiffling, Helen Shapiro
was still at school, the Beatles and the Stones were not around
yet, Sam Cooke and President Kennedy had not yet been shot
dead. Brigitte Bardot was twenty-seven and I was eight-and-a-
half. I had been brought up on Eric Coates's rousing hymn to the
Dam Busters and the bouncing bomb. But '61 was the summer of
'Blue Moon', in which Cornelius Harp, lead singer of the
Marcels, starts off standing alone without a dream in his heart,
without a love of his own, and two minutes later is no longer
alone, thanks to the beneficence of the blue moon. But it wasn't
the lyrics or even the sentiment which made an impression on me
so much as the backing, which continually explodes from behind
the scenes, soaring and swooping and swooning to eclipse the
lead: 'Dip-de-dip-dip-dip, bum-ba-ba-bum, ba-bum-ba-bum-
bum, bum-ba-bum-bum, dang-a-dang-dang, ding-a-dong-ding
. . .' This was, I imagine, what Jean-Jacques Rousseau had in
mind when he spoke of the *cri de la nature* that preceded fully
articulated language and gave direct and immediate expression
to raw emotion.

It was an age of innocence. Nonetheless there were distinct
tremors and rumblings, harbingers of a time that was not yet.

And the epicentre of those premonitory disturbances was the movie-star machine.

BB and I have led parallel lives. To begin with, we both have blonde hair (hers is dyed). She was born in Paris, I in London. My Riviera was the coast of Kent, my Mediterranean was the English Channel, and my St Tropez was Camber Sands. A few miles out of Rye, it was another country, an exotic land of mountainous sand dunes and pyramids which doubled as World War Two anti-tank fortifications, a peninsula, almost an island over which the law of England had no jurisdiction and from which there was no extradition, the refuge of bank robbers and master criminals, where we rented a holiday cottage we called the Shell House (because it was made of sea-shells; only much later did I realize there were a bare dozen scallops dotted around the front door) or camped in a caravan. My father used to say that on a clear day you could see France, but all I ever saw was the spit of land on the far side of the estuary, which I think was Kent.

Camber Sands was an Eden-by-the-sea which contained the seed of our inevitable corruption: the forbidden fruit-machine. In stately isolation at the end of a dirt track lay a vast amusement arcade, a shed the size of a transatlantic liner with a corrugated iron roof. Assorted sideshows – duck-shoot, test-your-strength, bowling alley – occupied its perimeter. There was a one-armed bandit that responded to a delicate touch with an almost guaranteed line of three strawberries and an instant profit of 2d.

If only we had stuck to the strawberries, my twin brother and I! But we were tempted by a glass-boxed crane that promised to wheel round and pick up some small but perfect object – a marble, a chewing gum, a toy soldier, a rubber snake – preciously encased in a plastic bubble and release it into a chute down which it would, in theory, slide into our fists. That crane was designed to thwart even the most expert of operators. Either the maw never closed tightly enough around the bubble, so that it would fall back among the foam, or if you ever did get it to snap shut, you would run out of time before you could shovel your loot down the exit and the crane swung back to neutral.

But our greatest extravagance and our downfall was the movie-star machine. How could we have resisted it? It was the focal point of our dreams, standing squarely in the centre of the arena, as rugged as a lighthouse. It was monumental, a colossus among slot-machines, a repository of arcane intricacies and deceits.

A miniature cathedral in the Perpendicular style in plastic and chrome, its north and south walls were grooved to house the idolatrous images of Jane Russell, Ava Gardner and Dorothy Lamour. Lamour was worth tuppence, Gardner 3d and Russell 4. Valued at a full sixpence was Marilyn Monroe. Lacking the experience and taste to make any discrimination on my own account, I accepted this hierarchy at face-value.

The face, and maybe a shadow of décolletage, was all I had to go on: four black-and-white portraits dominating the landscape like the presidents' heads on Mount Rushmore. There was a slot underneath where you slid in your penny homage and over their heads a bulb that lit up like a halo and conferred a blinding radiance on the face below, accompanied by a muted thunder-clap, the woof of a loudspeaker. On the same principle as roulette, the trick was to put your money on (or in) the one that would remain illuminated at the end of a circuit or two of lights flashing on and off. It was as if, by inserting your coin, you had to light the light of – Ava Gardner, for example. If you lost, and Gardner remained in darkness and someone else's light was lit, nothing to do with you, then you heard an empty dull thud; if you won, then you were rewarded by the tinkle of coppers sliding into the cup at the bottom. It was at this machine that I received my formative sexual education.

There was no escape. As the white lights over the heads of the quartet switched off, so four red lights at their waists switched on, silhouetting a sign which read PUT YOUR MONEY IN NOW in quadruplicate.

I was bound to favour Monroe: she paid up more rarely than the others – the tuppeny Lamour was, arithmetically, a better bet – but when she came through she came through in spades. The machine continued to function independently of human inter-vention, in accordance with its own iron-clad laws, and whole minutes could pass by without Monroe scooping the crown. I hungered for that maximum one-off pay-out, the silver sixpence, and was never content with merely accumulating small change. It was the jackpot or nothing. My brother, when he hadn't already dropped his shilling in the sand, played a more cautious game and often came away in credit; I was a long-term loser, but had a few moments of incalculable bliss to make up for my losses.

And then, in that summer of 1961, under the phantasmagoric translucency of a blue moon, Marilyn Monroe died. Or shortly before. Medically speaking, she clung to a remnant of life in Hollywood for another year or so before the coroner finally confirmed her demise. But by this time she was, in my eyes, already a phantom, her seeming flesh thin and transparent. For her existence on the movie-star machine had been abruptly terminated. When I got there in August she was gone. Her picture had been taken out and binned. Although I had no direct hand in her grisly fate, I still feel obscurely responsible, as if I had been sticking pins in a voodoo doll, and half expect to be denounced as the shadowy Mr Big lurking behind the Kennedys and the Mafia and the media moguls at the front of the culprits queue.

If I did not gloat over her passing, I did not mourn it either. For the vacancy she left behind had been instantly filled, filled to overflowing. I know (or thought I knew) that Brigitte Bardot was born on 28 September 1934 in her mother's bed in Paris, on the fifth floor of an apartment block in the Avenue de la Bourdonnais, barely 100 yards south-west of the Eiffel Tower. And yet I can never entirely relinquish the conviction that she emerged *ex nihilo*, in August 1961 at Camber Sands, rising up fully formed out of the valves and light-bulbs and sound-effects of the movie-star machine.

It was she then who was responsible for murdering Monroe. There was a kind of complicity between us. Too young for Marilyn, too old for Madonna, I was completely defenceless *vis-à-vis* BB. As with Mozart and Beethoven, so it is hard now to envisage Monroe and Bardot as overlapping. Chronologically, they coincided in the second half of the fifties: on 29 October 1956 they actually attended the same royal film première (of Michael Powell's *The Battle of the River Plate*) in Leicester Square, two of twenty to shake hands with the Queen; but semiotically they inhabit different worlds.

At first glance MM and BB have a lot in common. Blonde,

voluptuous, alliterative, iconic, mythified, they could almost have been cut from the same strip of celluloid. Bardot might have been mistaken for a reincarnation of Monroe, a phoenix emerging out of the barbiturates. If Monroe never appeared naked she nevertheless popped up on the beach from time to time, scantily clad. But the beach in question was likely to be Santa Monica, virtually a suburb of Hollywood. Monroe was born, brought up and died in Los Angeles, a child of 20th Century Fox from beginning to end. She was a studio creation, nothing but a projection, a serial image, flickering on the mental screen of the collective unconscious. It was not so much that she died too soon but rather that she was never truly alive. Tragic or comic, she was always a victim, carrying around the void inside her like an embryo. Like the ideational object dependent on a solipsist's perception, as soon as you stopped looking at her she ceased to exist.

Bardot, on the other hand, always exceeded the frame, the studio, the film. She was, in that specialized, existential sense, transcendent – quite independent of the perception we had of her. It was as if she had happened to pass before the lens, but was capable of moving on, never trapped by it. She was irreducible to her own images: elusive, dense, corporeal. Monroe had been oddly disembodied, unreal, condemned to fade and vanish long before she actually died, whereas BB was the unadorned incarnation of the carnal. The late Monroe was a pathological case, Bardot was emblematic of youthful wholesomeness.

All this was clear on the strength of my first glimpse of that 6d photograph at Camber Sands. The broad, slightly parted mouth, the swimming-pool eyes, the Niagara of hair, everything seemed to overrun the limits of the there-and-then, to rush away in other fabulous directions. Monroe had gone, but even Gardner, Russell and Lamour appeared visibly diminished, dimmed by the new arrival. Whether or not her light was lit, BB was luminous.

More than ever I felt the compulsion to blow my entire wad on the 6d. Everything in me rebelled against playing the percentages. And now there was an additional imperative to go for the maximum, born of a valuation that went well beyond any price-tag. Bardolatry had claimed another eight-year-old.

An incipient sense of morality whispered that fidelity would

13

surely be rewarded and kept me broadly loyal to the new woman in my life. Still, from time to time, the suspicion that I was, in all probability, throwing my money away, would drive me to flirt now with Lamour, now with Russell, or even turn back to the strawberry certainties of the fruit machines. It was my father who forced me into making a serious commitment.

Our time at Camber was nearly up; it was the end of the afternoon, time to go back for tea, and for some reason we were on our own. I bullied him into taking me into the arcade. He only had a sixpence on him by way of change, which we converted into pennies at the counter.

'What one do you think, Dad?'

'That's up to you, son. You choose.'

Like surfers scrutinizing the waves before they paddle out, my brother and I had often had the feeling that if it were only possible to contemplate the sequence of illuminations long enough, then we would be able to comprehend the whole cosmic pattern as it recurred eternally, grasping its general principles of order and justice, and that we would be able to ride our luck and coast in.

But that afternoon I was rushed. PUT YOUR MONEY IN *NOW*. I rammed my penny into the slot around Bardot's waist and released it.

*Whumpa-whumpa-whumpa-whumpa-whumpa.* LAMOUR.

My left hand took another penny from my right hand and shoved it in again. It was like taking penalties: the second time round the goalie is expecting you to shoot for the opposite corner, so you put the ball in the exact same spot and send him the wrong way.

*Whumpa-whumpa-whumpa-whumpa.* LAMOUR.

Unless, of course, the goalie expects you to expect him to expect you will go the other way, so he goes the same way. Third time lucky though.

*Whumpa-whumpa-whumpa-whumpa-whumpa-whumpa.*
RUSSELL.

Bitch. I was half-way through my pile and starting to get nervous. My father hovered around my shoulder. Down to threepence. I needed to hit the jackpot to show any kind of margin. And I couldn't pull out now, it would have been rank

14

cowardice under fire. I plugged in another coin and gave it my lucky push.

*Whumpa-whumpa*. LAMOUR.

Lamour was having an incredible run, but even if I'd plumped for the sloe-eyed sultry look I'd still have felt short-changed in comparison with the hypothetical riches Bardot promised to bestow on me. If I switched now, I would be cursing myself when Bardot finally came up. And what was I going to switch to anyway? Lamour again? Impossible. Gardner? Russell? Unlikely. No, Bardot was no longer the longshot, the risky improbability, but the solid bet among the four. This time, I couldn't lose.

*Whumpa-whumpa-whumpa-whumpa-whumpa-whumpa*. RUSSELL.

One measly penny left. But still there was the chance of multiplying it into six and restoring the original bequest intact into the hand of my father. I fell back on my most ingenious strategy, a last resort which had never been known to fail. Despair. Assume defeat, anticipate disaster – and it wouldn't happen. The trick was to rule out in advance all thought that Bardot would win, and then she would.

OK. This time it would be Gardner for sure. *Gardner*, I muttered under my breath. *Gardner*, and squeezed that bulging coin down the 6d hole. *Money down the drain*, I said to myself. Flushing it away, down the plughole, down the pan, down, down, down.

*Whumpa-whumpa-whumpa-whumpa-whumpa-whumpa-whumpa*. GARDNER.

I was numb, dumbfounded. Quite who had won I wasn't sure, but I knew I had lost 6–0. I was so crushed I forgot even to blackmail another sixpence out of my father. The sickening realization came upon me that I hadn't repressed the hope of winning wholeheartedly enough. That was the explanation: I still secretly saw myself trousering those six pennies that would have slid down out of Bardot and into the cup. Fool! Fool! Fool! Justly punished for such surreptitious presumption. Or, on second thoughts, had the machine spotted my ploy, and compensated accordingly? Or was it – the idea astonished me – that I had conquered hope so absolutely that I had actually brought about what I had, only strategically, been wishing for? I could control the machine after all. But it was too late. Clearly, I should have openly gambled on Bardot, stated my allegiance, backed it, predicted the outcome explicitly, and won. I should have had faith. I had learned my lesson.

'Bad luck, son. Better luck next time, eh?'

It wasn't luck, or the lack of it. I was responsible. It was my fault. I still feel a distant pang of guilt on this account, even though I have plenty of other things to feel guiltier about, and on certain nights the recollection of this trauma is enough to awaken me, sweating and tearful. After all, I had just tossed away a small fortune, the entire contents of my father's pockets, on a woman. This was my twisted primal scene. My father observing me having sex with a machine. For money. And it didn't even fake an orgasm.

## 3

# 24 October 1963 and One Afternoon in April the Same Year

Ce que finalement je sais de plus sûr sur la morale et les obligations des hommes, c'est au foot que je le dois.

Albert Camus

(Ultimately all that I know most surely about morality and the obligations of man I know from football.)

All she had to do was walk in through a door, and then walk out of it again. Enter and exit; in, out. Perhaps it was some faintly apprehended allegory of sexual penetration that caused the riot. But then again perhaps not, since she never got as far as the garden gate.

The door was in Flask Walk in Hampstead. The film was *Adorable Idiot* with Anthony Perkins as a Russian spy. Bardot ('Agent 38–24–36') was scheduled to start filming at 2.15 pm. By the time she actually arrived, at 4 pm, a 500–strong crowd (some reports put the figure at more like 1,000) had gathered. Despite substantial police reinforcements and a director clamouring through a megaphone for 'English phlegm', hundreds of stiff upper lips loosened up and ran amok on the set. An espionage movie, even a spoof-spook flick, soon becomes impossible with enough uninvited extras on board to shoot *Waterloo*. Though London had previously witnessed Sophia Loren, Gina Lollobrigida, Jayne Mansfield, even Marilyn Monroe enter its gates and film openly on its streets, it yet remained impassive, indifferent, icy. It took BB to induce meltdown. Eventually a fake London complete with bowler-hats and oddly attired policemen, but without Englishmen, had to be constructed in Paris where filming could be conducted in an atmosphere of artistic tranquillity and sexual satiation.

Revisionist historians are apt to dismiss the whole thing as a fake, a brazen publicity stunt, orchestrated, choreographed and stage-managed from beginning to end. The cameras would have had no film in them. There would never have been any intention to shoot on location. The crowd – consisting, in any case, mostly of press photographers and reporters – would, wittingly or not, have participated in some cunning PR conspiracy to bamboozle us into believing that BB was nuclear enough to send tremors through the otherwise rigid and repressive sensibility of Phileas Fogg and his compatriots.

From my own point of view, it wasn't so much that the fans got in the way of filming as that the films tended to invade the more intimate rapport of star and fan. I have no recollection of the film, but the day Hampstead caught fire is synaptically lodged in my brain. The secondary was becoming primary. Art was being swiftly displaced by life; or, what amounted to the same thing, life was being infiltrated by art. In short, BB's films were already hard pushed to keep up with the fantasy of reality.

And whether or not the ostensibly unscripted Flask Walk scene was itself ultimately scripted, the sense of an emotional renaissance (or naissance) in England was genuine. I had already witnessed a mirror-image of this some months earlier, towards the end of my junior school career in the dying days of the football season.

Technically, the match against St Ursula's was of small importance. It wasn't a cup-tie and neither side was in contention for league honours. It wasn't even a bitterly fought local derby or grudge game with scores to be settled. It was almost a friendly, an exercise in style, ballet with balls. I was playing in goal in those days, the position honourably occupied by Albert Camus before his car hit a tree in January 1960.

I can't recall exactly how the goal came about. Was it a long shot that floated over my head? (Since I was then less than five feet tall and the bar was over seven, I was at a disadvantage with the lofted ball.) Or did their nippy inside-left run rings around the defence and then humiliatingly slip it through my legs? All I clearly recollect was the aftermath. As a rule our own scorers would trot dutifully back to our half so the game could resume. At most they would be met with a rugged handshake or a quiet word of congratulation. Getting your name on the score-sheet was reward and remembrance enough.

The St Ursulan no. 10, in contrast, was rushed, surrounded, clasped, his stupid freckles and cissy ginger curls kissed, swamped, swallowed up. The scrum was formed less of his team-mates than of an ardent mob of girls with a rare enthusiasm for the game. It was my first pitch invasion, the kind of thing I associated with Brazil, not Romford. At this rate St Ursula's would soon be needing a moat and an electrified fence. And even then I would have expected some of the fans to impale themselves on the barbed wire like would-be escapees traversing the Berlin Wall in their passion to embrace freedom.

There was a lot of screaming, I remember. If there was any dialogue it was incomprehensible to me, like the scene itself. It must have been later on that someone told me that the name of the kid who scored was Griffin.

# 4

## Midnight, One Night in January 1968

BB: Je ferai tout ce que tu voudras.

*Et Dieu créa la femme*

(I'll do everything you want me to.)

It is now a practically forgotten footnote in the annals of musical history that Brigitte Bardot, not Jane Birkin, was Serge Gainsbourg's first choice as partner to record 'Je t'aime, moi non plus.' He wrote it for her. They recorded it together at midnight in January 1968, behind closed doors, without a band. Word soon got around that it was the sound of Gainsbourg and Bardot making love. Birkin – his then wife – was an afterthought. Oddly, Bardot and Birkin would end up singing the song to one another in 1973, stripped naked on the set of *Don Juan, ou Et si Don Juan était une femme*, before shooting a lesbian scene.

Griffo and I blamed Birkin on Sachsy. He it was who, having heard BB's respiratory harmonizing with Gainsbourg, squashed its release and had the master disc locked up in the archives, gagged, manacled, strait-jacketed and welded into a lead coffin then buried at the bottom of the soundless soundproofed sea, whence, many years later, it would make its Houdini-like escape and finally reach my hungering ears. It was like trying to get rid of plutonium waste – ultimately the radiation would seep out and contaminate us all. But, in the short-term, Gainsbourg had to fall back on Birkin. All in all there's no knowing how many candidates for aural sex he ran through.

In his book *Les Stars*, the French sociologist Edgar Morin recognizes that 'true fans anticipate the divorce from the very moment of a star's marriage'. In some cases this is true of the stars themselves. Bardot and Sachs married in a fit of nostalgia for a passion that had already died. Privy as we were to BB's innermost thoughts and feelings, we knew for a certainty that Sachs's days were numbered. It was all there in *Shalako*, for example, where backwoodsman Sean Connery has no difficulty in wresting the Countess Irina (BB) from the anaemic Sachs-substitute Count Friedrich. But our prescience was not derived merely from seeing her on screen. As Hortense Powdermaker observes in *Hollywood: The Dream Factory*, 'the relationship of fans to their stars is not limited to seeing them in movies, any more than primitive people's relationship to their totemic heroes is limited to hearing a myth told occasionally.' In truth, we were largely ignorant of the canon of actual performances. But we were word-perfect in the collected gossip columns of *Tit-Bits*, *Reveille*, the *Daily Express*, the *Daily Mail* and the *News of the World*, versed in the language of the tabloids even before they were tabloids. BB was forever talking exclusively, frankly, 'as she has never talked before'. Posters, stills, newsreels framed our imaginings. Sitting around in Stones Coffee Bar, we would analyse the reasons for Sachsy's inevitable fall from grace, parodying the cheap headlines which were our Bible.

'The Kraut Is Out.'

'The Hun Is Done.'

'How about this then? Sachs Cracks.'

'Nice.'

How could we not resent and loathe and envy and admire the bugger? He spent Christmas at St Moritz and New Year in Gstaad, drinking *Glühwein* on the Wassengrat. We spent Christmas and New Year in Romford, drinking lager and lime at the Coopers and watery Nescaff at Stones. His name had been linked, we knew, with the lovely Princess Soraya, the loaded Tina Onassis and Marina Doria, world water-skiing champion. He had saved the life of Birgitta Laaf, the Swedish model, beautiful but crippled, by coming up with a surgeon to cure her spinal tumour. His first wife had died tragically young. He had it all, except for Bardot. Then he had Bardot.

Serge Marquand, the younger brother of Christian Marquand (BB's *homme fatal* in *And God Created Woman*), made the mistake of introducing Bardot to the man with the Bauhaus face at the Vieille Fontaine restaurant in St Tropez. She was having an affair with (a) handsome Brazilian promoter, Bob Zagury, and (b) her dentist, Paul Albou, at the time. But the dental surgeon was off in Paris poking around in other women's mouths and Zagury was almost a kilometre away. And on that balmy summer's evening, she was sitting just a few yards from Sachs at an adjoining table.

'You seem to have been avoiding me for the last ten years,' Gunther complained.

'I hadn't noticed,' Bardot shot back.

They danced together at Papagayo and there are those who maintain that she spent that night and the next at La Capilla, Sachs's St Tropez estate. I like to think she put up a shade more resistance than that. How else to explain the Blitzkrieg that followed? The one hundred dozen red roses that arrived on her doorstep the next morning, tossed out of a helicopter; the £50,000 the lucky sod won at Monte Carlo and then lavished on her? BB was assaulted, invaded, annexed. It must have been like trying to hold back a column of Panzer tanks.

Handsome Brazilian promoter Bob Zagury (what he promoted no one knew), who fondly imagined he was going to be sleeping with Bardot, was left waiting at La Madrague for her to come home. 'I thought she was shopping in Paris,' he is supposed to have said when he heard the news. 'She didn't mention any wedding plans to me.'

Eventually BB gathered her forces and staged a fightback, conducting her guerrilla campaign through the press, where she confirmed our hopes about their incompatibility.

'I give myself entirely, but he lives on compromises and is incapable of giving up his past. He tries to take me into a social world that I detest and have always done my best to avoid.'

'Typical sodding Nazi!' Griffo slammed a fist into the palm of his other hand, as I read on greedily.

'Our tastes are so different. He loves everything luxurious, loud, and he loves photographers and publicity. When he gives me a present it has to be a grandiose one, while I would prefer a key-ring chosen with love.'

'Now you're talking – I'll give you a key-ring!'

Perhaps she was thinking of Mike Sarne at the time, but she spoke to us. BB frowned on the kind of profligacy which was beyond us anyway. She publicly hymned exactly the kind of privacy we also had in mind. We took comfort from the report that she refused to share the Sachs apartment on the Avenue Foch, which she openly ridiculed as 'the Gunther Hilton' and where all the beautiful leather-bound books turned out to be bought by the yard, pure decor, and included a *History of Nineteenth-Century Dentistry*. That was the Boche for you. We knew it would not be long before husband no. 3 went the way of nos 1 and 2, and although he and BB would not be officially divorced until 1969, we had long since bracketed him out of her life. Banning the disc of 'Je t'aime' was not going to stop BB giving voice, and indeed body, to that endearment, nor stop us vibrating along with her.

The fact that BB's original was suppressed only served to make it all the more incendiary in our over-heated imaginations. 'Je t'aime moi non plus' was the perfect song for her, the exact musical analogue of the woman. There was no ambiguity about its message: no irony, no end-of-the-pier, dirty-postcard innuendo: its panting, sighing, semi-asthmatic sonorities were a three-minute warning of coital rapture. And the semantics of BB were similarly transparent: to our eyes, there was no distinction (to put the matter in Saussurean terms) between her signifier and her signified: she was nothing but sex, she was solid sex through and through, an immense, living, walking, breathing biology textbook.

As Marguerite Duras wrote (in 1964), 'When a man attracts her, Bardot goes straight to him. Nothing stops her. It does not matter if she is in a café, at home or staying with friends. She goes off with him on the spot without a glance at the man she is leaving. In the evening perhaps she will come back, perhaps not.' Her sentiments were oddly echoed by a Dominican priest, Father Marie-Dominique Bouyer, in an open letter to BB published in the *Vie catholique illustrée* in 1966: 'In eight minutes you got married again in Las Vegas. You no longer belong to M. Vadim, nor to M. Charrier, nor to M. Zaguri: you belong to M. Sachs. In eight minutes you swear faithfulness for life. If someone else comes on the scene tomorrow whom you do not know today, will you get married again?' There was no contradiction in her inconsistency. As Bardot herself explained (in 1975), 'When I say to a man: "I love you," then I love him. It does not mean, however, that I shall also love him the next day. I may change my mind. In love nothing is fixed. What was true an hour ago is now no longer true.' Till death do us part; a day; an hour: the duration of love was contracting, shrinking down to the length of a song, towards zero, promising the maximum in the minimum.

We could hear the diaphragm of BB rising and falling, rising and falling. Her words were addressed directly to us:

*Tu es la vague, moi l'île nue*
*Tu vas, tu vas et tu viens*
*Entre mes reins.*
(You are the wave, I am the naked island, you go, you go and you come between my loins.)

This was not a trope, not poetry – more an objective technical analysis of the act of copulation. This is the way things really were, all islands and waves and a relentless unfurling on the shore. If we'd had no grasp of French whatever, there would still have been no danger of our not getting the drift. Even so, lying on his bed, in the naked shadow of BB on the beach at St Trope, beside the poster of Otis Redding (the publicity shot for 'Sitting on the Dock of the Bay'), with his record player spinning, Griffo questioned some of my translations.

'*Je t'aime*, OK, got it: *I love you*. But this *moi non plus* business?'

Griffo had the hair of a red setter and the face of Paul McCartney. He could stick posters of Brigitte and Otis on his bedroom wall, whereas my parents retained strict copyright over every magnolia inch of plaster. He could pull the most gormless face in the whole of the British Isles, guaranteed to put the wind up old ladies. He could still pass for fourteen and go half-price on the buses even when he could already pass for eighteen and drink himself into a slobbering, vomiting stupor. He could enunciate *fuck*, *shit*, *cunt* and *shag* without blinking and make those pervasive monosyllables seem like the elusive and indispensable *mot juste*. Griffo had it all. Except for Bardot.

'"Me neither. Neither do I." Clever, isn't it?'

'I still don't get it.' Griffo was not alone. The Gainsbourg refrain had been laughably mistranslated in the pop music

24

columns as 'I don't love you any more,' or, even worse, 'None more than me.'

'It's a paradox,' I explained. 'There's no such thing as "love" – not in any romantic sense. He is acknowledging that she doesn't really mean anything by it.'

'So when you say, "I love you," it's really like saying "hello", is that it?'

'Or "nice day", that sort of thing: it's just a formality, a rhetorical move. You've still got sex though: *un amour physique, sans issue* – without consequences, not leading anywhere, no kids.' Fortunately, I had taken the precaution of bringing along my Harraps dictionary just to be on the safe side.

We would groan along with the record and were particularly keen to imitate Gainsbourg's gravelly rendition of *Je vais, je vais et je viens entre tes reins* (that 'between your kidneys' took a lot of patient deciphering), but we agreed it would take decades of Gauloises even to get close. We took careful note that although the woman passes from breathing to moaning and comes close to screaming in ecstasy by the end, the man confines himself to something resembling a polite cough. Altogether we learned a lot from that record.

'*Je t'aime*, Griffo,' I said.

'*Moi non plus*,' Griffo said, fluently.

'How's about playing along a bit here and saying, *Moi aussi*?'

'Or what about "Get 'em off, darling"? How do you say that?'

'Technically, *Ote tes vêtements* ought to do it. Assuming the familiar form of address. Which I think we can assume by this stage. Or *Dévêts-toi*. Unclothe thyself, literally.'

# 5

## Spring 1968

JUDGE: On vous voit dans les cafés, vous allez jusqu'à trois
fois par semaine au cinéma. Cette vie de dissipation
aboutit très rapidement sa conséquence logique – vous
prenez un amant.

*La Vérité*

(You are seen in cafés, you go to the cinema up to three
times a week. This life of dissipation leads very rapidly
to its logical conclusion – you take a lover.)

In the works of Jules Verne there are certain *points suprêmes* (as
Michel Butor has called them) which exert a compulsive force
over his travellers. They are the poles, the centre of the earth and
the moon. By 1968 the location of these sacred sites had shifted,
but all paths to transcendence still boiled down to three. We
could head west and fry our brains with LSD in Haight Ashbury.
We could follow the hippy trail to the East and find spiritual
enlightenment in Kathmandu. Otherwise, we could take the
Autoroute du Sud direct to St Tropez, the belt of blinding white
sand that hitched the ochre earth of Provence to the wine-dark
sea, an itinerary as quick and as cheap as an injection straight
into the vein, with no risk of long-term dependency.

Such was the conclusion Griffo and I arrived at in Stones. In
*Being and Nothingness* Jean-Paul Sartre writes, 'It is certain that
the café by itself, with its patrons, its tables, its booths, its
mirrors, its light, its smokey atmosphere, and the sounds of
voices, rattling saucers and footsteps which fill it – the café is a
plenitude of being.' Stones had plenitude all right. It had nothing
to do with the Rolling Stones; there was no question of going
there to get stoned. L. F. Stone and Sons Ltd was the family
company (absorbed eventually into the Debenhams empire) that

26

created the clean, anonymous, middle-class department store where my mother sold Singer sewing machines under the escalator on the ground floor. It didn't matter whether you wanted one or not, she sold you one all the same. There was a man who only bent down to tie his shoelaces and when he straightened up again he found a brand new sewing machine tucked under his arm. The cafeteria near the back exit was furnished with a self-service counter and steaming stainless steel cylinders and a disapproving grey-haired matron at the till in a white cap embroidered with the name STONES. Stones was our Deux Magots, our Café Flore.

In the very same September that Sarne bedded Bardot, the Oxford Institute of Experimental Psychology published a study by its Social Skills Research Group comparing how many 'contacts' (hand-holding, hair-stroking, kissing, fondling, etc.) took place per hour in cafés around the world. Mexico City came top of the class with 180; Paris was second with 120. London scored 0. Romford had dropped off the bottom of the scale.

It was from Stones, our vantage point on the south side of Romford Market, that we threw ourselves into the feverish political and sexual struggles of the sixties and dreamed – even without having read, without needing to read – Herbert Marcuse's dream of a rapprochement between eros and civilization. Upstairs was a straitlaced waitress-served restaurant called the Verandah, which overlooked the fashion floor and where mannequins would parade for customers who could eat and buy at the same time; we stayed true to our libidinous roots on the ground floor, the refuge of dissidents and deadbeats.

It was here that we fell in with a plan to join a protest against the Vietnam War in Grosvenor Square, but our hearts weren't really in it from the moment the two highly motivated sisters who invited us along threw up the barricades when we tried to storm them. It was in Stones that we were once arrested on suspicion of theft and our street credibility rocketed.

In Stones every fat man with a doughnut and a cup of tea was SS or the Inquisition, and our every whispered insult was a symbolic blow for freedom. I remember when Jeff Jerome, in his mauve bandanna and bleached Levis with the pink polka-dot flares sewn into the seams, went out to have his teeth kicked in by

27

some pushers who felt he owed them, taking the precaution of popping a couple of uppers beforehand so he wouldn't feel the pain; when I tried to collar Eva Szczepanska – lying my age up a few crucial months – from right under the nose of Kevin Baxter who played centre-half for the First XI; when Griffo faced up to the challenge of Margaret Vickers, the classiest bird in Romford.

But as Sartre also wrote, nothingness pervades being. Being generates nothingness. A sense of lack interjected itself between our gaze and the Formica-covered table-tops and orange vinyl benches, and we discovered non-being and emptiness and nausea lying in wait like sludge at the bottom of our coffee cups. Girls rushed in to fill the vacuum.

The geisha girl, painted and polished perfection, was a fad of Griffo's for a while. Then after my holiday at Lloret de Mar on the Costa Brava it was Spanish girls, filleted at birth and nothing but flesh through and through. At one stage Griffo went through a Sophia Loren phase and couldn't believe it when she married Carlo bloody Ponti, a fat midget who was not man enough for her, and she'd be needing other outlets for her passion, she would. (We had cause to be grateful to Ponti, however, when as producer of *Le Mépris* he persuaded Jean-Luc Godard to add a nude BB scene.) Loren and Ekberg, Gina Lollobrigida, Ursula Andress, Claudia Cardinale, each might have qualified as the 'id' girl. But promiscuous though we were, we kept coming back to BB.

Waiting in the café for Pierre to turn up, sipping frugally at his ersatz Occupation coffee and chewing on cheap cigarettes, Sartre apprehends that 'the absent Pierre haunts this café' and that, by not being there, he annihilates being. So it was for Griffo and me, possessed and yet not possessed by Brigitte Bardot. Stones was permeated, perfumed, percolated by her absence.

Our love for her was fundamentally Platonic. But it is a fallacy to think of Plato's eros as something cool or abstract or second-order. In the dialogues of Plato, Socrates has many conversations which go roughly like this:

SOCRATES: What is the beautiful (*to kalon*)?
ALCIBIADES: A beautiful maiden is beautiful.
SOCRATES: Yes. But I asked not what is beautiful, but what the beautiful is.

ALCIBIADES: A beautiful boy then. A boy is more beautiful than a maiden.

SOCRATES: But is not the beautiful boy or maiden ugly compared to the gods?

ALCIBIADES: Well, yes – compared to the gods.

SOCRATES: But the absolutely beautiful must be that which is beautiful to all and will never appear ugly anywhere to anybody.

Thus he leads Alcibiades (or Hippias or one of the other idle dossers hanging about the Stones of Athens) to his concept of the Form or Idea of Beauty, the beautiful in itself (*to auto kalon*), which is exempt from worldly imperfections; and to his mind-blowing formula: 'Beautiful things are made beautiful by beauty.' Just as the particular table or chair that we see before us has been fashioned by reference to the Table or the Chair which exists in some supra-sensory realm, and that which is true or good is so in the light of the True and the Good, so too the beautiful woman is beautiful as a reflection of the Form of Beauty or the Beautiful.

Aristotle's refutation of Plato, a classic *reductio ad absurdum*, rests not on a woman but a man: specifically, the Third Man. A man is recognized as a man because he resembles the Man, the archetype, of necessity beautiful since all the Forms participate in the Beautiful (and the True and the Good). But if there is a resemblance then the Man is also, in some aspect, *a* man. Following the same argument, he too is recognizable as a man only by reference to some other archetype of the archetype, or the Third Man; the Third Man implies a fourth, the fourth a fifth, and so on, in an infinite regression of beautiful men. Therefore, there is no such thing as *the* Woman, the Beautiful, the True, the Good, but only individual beautiful women, true propositions, good deeds and so on, and all our general concepts are formed out of particular perceptions rather than the reverse. Aristotle would not have believed in the hazy sub-Platonic concept of the Most Beautiful Woman in the World.

But we did. I suspect most of us try to be good Aristotelians, but the perspective of an infinite number of beautiful women is too terrifying, and we fall back into Platonism. We cannot tolerate too much beauty. We hanker after the Form, the model, the archetype, by reference to which all other women are perceived as imitations. The title of *The Good, the Bad, and the Ugly*, the Sergio Leone/Clint Eastwood film (1968), illustrates the prevalence at the time of neo-platonist thinking. In Greek terms, the Good and the Beautiful are synonymous or, more precisely, 'the Beautiful is father to the Good' (*Phaedo*, 345). Aesthetics precedes ethics.

Griffo and I were – maybe all fifteen-year-olds are – neo-platonic extremists, raving fundamentalists of Bardogma.

ANDY: Who's the most beautiful chick you can think of?
GRIFFO: Sandie Emerson.
ANDY: Who is Sandie Emerson?
GRIFFO: Jimmy Emerson's sister.
ANDY: But she's not as beautiful as Brigitte Bardot, is she? She's ugly compared to Brigitte Bardot.
GRIFFO: She's the Brigitte Bardot of Romford.

We were desperate for a First Cause, the *primum mobile* of the cosmos. And in BB we had found one. She was the archetype reified, she was a heaven that could be accessed here below, she was £200 that could be collected without the necessity of passing Go.

We were not alone in our choice. Sartre says somewhere that when you choose you choose for all men. We had the feeling that every other man on the planet was rolling along with us on this one. BB was universally recognized as the Woman. In the words of Italian songster Michelino, *Apparve sullo scherm' e tutto il mondo sospira* ('She appeared on the screen and the whole world gave a sigh'), *La la la la la la la lai lai lai lai lai lai Brigit-te Bar-dot Bar-dot Brigit-te Bar-dot Bar-dot BB BB BB no no no no no no tutti matti tutti matti di Bardot*. Bob Dylan, aged fifteen, dedicated his first love-song to BB. Griffo was never a Dylan man, so it was by chance at Jel Strudwick's house that I came across *The Freewheelin' Bob Dylan*, an album from the early sixties that contained the track, 'I Shall be Free'. I leapt up to wrench the pickup back and home in on the part where Dylan takes a call from President Kennedy:

My friend, Bob (says Kennedy), what do we need to make the country grow?

My friend, John (replies Dylan): Brigitte Bardot.

I passed on this insight to Griffo. We tried out a few rhymes of our own involving 'go', 'flow', 'blow' and 'yo-ho-ho'. But we agreed that the United States of America and for that matter Romford definitely needed Brigitte Bardot if we were going to grow. She was our vitamin BB. For good measure, Dylan chipped in 'Anita Ekberg . . . Sophia Loren . . . Country'll grow!', but they didn't rhyme.

In *Babette s'en va-t-en guerre* (1959), an Oxford psychologist parachutes the blonde bombshell into occupied France, turning theories of genetic supremacy back against the Nazis and unleashing her on the German High Command. According to Michelino, 'No one yet knows why she pleases me, why she pleases you.' But psychology acknowledges the existence of an 'objective universal', that set of features – a specific configuration of big eyes and high cheekbones, a certain ratio of waist to hips, the quintessence of optimal fertility – that is programmed into our DNA and guaranteed to trigger our reproductive behaviour: a set of stimuli that automatically induces an inescapable response. Psychology insists, however, that the objective universal is only a concept, a geometry, an impossible symmetry, like the triangle and the circle, that does not exist in reality. But by the end of the fifties Brigitte Bardot had, for all practical purposes, become indistinguishable from the objective universal.

Of course there were bound to be other claimants to the throne. Sometimes it would be a toss-up between Bardot and Ekberg. 'Anita, Anita,' Griffo would moan, 'Mam-ma mia!' Both, we knew, had a fondness for fifteen-year-old boys. In fact, they couldn't keep their hands off fifteen-year-olds. Show them a fifteen-year-old boy and there'd be no stopping them. This was common knowledge among fifteen-year-olds at the time. There was no question, fifteen was the ideal age to be.

BB had one advantage over her rivals. While the pretenders dwelt in some remote Hollywood empyrean, BB alone had given out not just her statistics but her co-ordinates. We might toy with the idea of going off to rendezvous with Raquel, but the truth was we didn't have a clue which way to go. BB had supplied a map and directions.

We knew – along with a billion or so other interested parties – that she lived in a sleepy fishing village on the Riviera, behind the high whitewashed walls of her secluded villa, La Madrague, where she lay beside the topaz pool in the purple shade of the bougainvillea.

*La Madrague*. It was the name of dozens of villas dotted along the Mediterranean coast. But its etymology seemed, in BB's case, uncannily apt. In the Provençal dialect, the *madraga*, derived from the Arabic *almazraba*, 'pregnant', was a multi-tiered rope net that once was looped across the mouths of open bays to catch unwary tuna, swordfish and shark. The netkeeper's cottage, by metonymy, came to be known as La Madrague, a kind of French Fisherman's Rest. Now *la drague* referred to the business of hooking and reeling in a human catch.

In the fifties, a previous generation had been called up for military service. With us it was BB. This was a draft we could not dodge. In the summer of 1968 it was reasonable to suppose that all we had to do was turn up on the beach at St Tropez and volunteer. We didn't have to find her: she would find us.

We weren't naive. We weren't going into this with our eyes closed. We weren't planning to *marry* Bardot. We knew – witness the case of Mike Sarne – that our chances of lasting the week were practically zero. *Haine, amour et trahison* ('hate, love and betrayal' – a 1954 Italian production in which BB played the spoils of war) were our lot. So be it. We expected no more – but no less.

# 6

## Summer 1956, Winter 1967

Merveilleux le cinéma. On voit des femmes, elles ont des robes, elles font du cinéma, crac! on voit leur cul.

*Le Mépris*

(Cinema is wonderful. You see some women with their clothes on, they go into films and – pow! – you see their arses.

*Contempt*)

The question is: can you ever see a woman completely naked? Griffo reckoned his sister, Kathleen, getting out of the bath was about as completely naked as he ever hoped to see. When I stayed the night at his place, we would leave the door of his bedroom open in the hopes of seeing her stride by unrobed as we lay there, from her bedroom on the right to the bathroom on the left. One night we got our wish. Silhouetted against the banisters, Kathleen passed briefly and for ever in front of our eyes, all belly, bum and spheroid breasts in perfect harmony, her cylindrical nipples glowing like cigarettes in the darkness.

Beyond that, we were restricted to glimpses, snatches, flashes of thigh or tit, fractions of the whole, thrown back on wide-ranging phallogocentrism to supplement our patchy perceptions. It was not until I read Roland Barthes's *Le Plaisir du texte* in the seventies that I discovered the aesthetics of the fragmentary and the partial, that 'pleasure resides in intermittence', and that the most intense pleasure could be derived from the yawning gap between one garment and another. Back then it was all or nothing.

BB was naked. She was lying on the beach, half in half out of the water, back to the Mediterranean sun. Her legs, like the bottom half of a mermaid, vanished into the sea, lapped by the surf. Her torso rested on the wet sand. Her long blonde tresses, curled and crinkled with salt, splashed down over her back. Her breasts, which could be seen as she arched her back, echoed the mounds of her buttocks. A single line ran from her neck, dipping and rising through hills and valleys, right down to her toes. In colour, she looked as if she had been dipped in butter and slowly toasted over a flame.

The poster taped to Griffo's bedroom wall was a publicity still from *And God Created Woman* (primitive versions resorted to painting in a bikini). Bardot was the first perfectly naked woman I never saw. How could the image of her not remain with me for ever? As I remember it, the camera catches her by accident. There is no foreplay with the lens, no teasing, no gradual unpeeling or build-up. Immersed *in medias res*, we see a woman who conceals nothing. Devoid of contradiction or irony or deception, she radiated the shattering truth that what you see is what you get.

Sexual intercourse was invented in 1963, Philip Larkin said, some time between the Lady Chatterley trial and the Beatles' first LP. The news didn't reach us until late 1967, when we saw *And God Created Woman*. Our occasional forays into Soho cinemas had been uniformly disappointing. Titles like *Milkmaids*, or *Schoolgirls on Parade*, or *Confessions of a Windowcleaner*, announced an authoritative account of the crux. But a diet of pigtails and stiletto heels, black stockings and suspender belts was deficient, particularly when dubbed from the Danish. You could see more at the public baths. In fact we did see more at the public baths, and spent a lot of spare time there, martyrs to chlorine.

*And God Created Woman* was showing in the late slot at the Gaumont, now an eight-lane Tesco's. I have heard that the mother superior of a convent in France took a bunch of novices along to see it, in the expectation of an edifying outing, since it had 'God' in the title. Similarly we went because it included the word 'woman'. But we too anticipated some biblical epic. And that, turned through ninety degrees, was how we saw it. Every close-up was an epiphany. Even with her clothes on BB was naked. It could only have taken about fifteen seconds to conclude that Charlton Heston was dead.

That nun would never have made her interpretative gaffe had she but studied the corollary spelt out on the poster: 'But the devil invented Bardot!' We were uplifted to learn that the Roman Catholic Legion of Decency condemned the film as 'an open violation of Christian and traditional morality' and that Juliette had been thrown out of the orphanage for refusing to supply a certificate of virginity. Monsignor James T. Lyng of Lake Placid, upstate New York, offered $250 from his own pocket to have it removed from his local cinema. The Vatican then forbade Catholics to visit this unholy place for six months after it had shown the film. In Germany riot police were summoned. In Sweden a young man cut his wrists in the balcony and bled over the cheaper seats downstairs. In England a couple divorced on the grounds that the husband preferred virtual sex with Bardot to the real thing with his wife. Another man wrote to the Problems Page of a national newspaper complaining of a tendency to cry out 'Brigitte!' very loudly at the climax of love-making. The agony aunt recommended that he find himself a new girl named Brigitte. It was the only solution.

There is an exchange between a soldier and a revolutionary in Mario Vargas Llosa's novel *The Real Life of Alejandro Mayta*, set in Peru at the beginning of the sixties, which contains these lines: '"Did you see *And God Created Woman*, with Brigitte Bardot?" asked Vallejos. "I saw it yesterday. Long legs, so long they come right out of the screen. I'd like to go to Paris someday and see Brigitte Bardot in the flesh."' Setting aside the obvious solecism – the silly bugger would sail all the way over from South America only to draw a blank in Paris while we were hot on her tail in St Tropez – this same conversation was taking place all over the world off and on from one end of the decade to the other. The global illusion was that we had all already seen her in the flesh.

Juliette was Brigitte and Brigitte was Juliette. She promised us everything. I swear I remember her diving in and out of bed with a multitude of lovers, seemingly indifferent to identity. 'The story,' Donald Zec enthused in a preview in the *Daily Mirror*, 'is of a fisherman's wanton daughter whose affairs were nearly as numerous as the pebbles on the beach.' She is an animal, spontaneous, impulsive, with no thought beyond the gratification of desire. She has the courage to do what she wants when

35

she wants (as Curd Jurgens/Carradine says in the movie). Now I am shocked to discover that she (a) makes love to only two men, one of them her husband (the other his brother), and (b) returns, in the end, to the conjugal bed of Jean-Louis Trintignant. He slaps her brutally, she smiles and slinks off, subdued: the phenomenal force has been tamed. Such is the conventional 'happy ending' of the film. But such is the impact of everything that precedes it that it surely cannot last. Juliette is never going to make a model wife and mother. When Michel/Trintignant declares that he is to marry Juliette, Antoine laughs his head off.

'Never has so much been shown to so many' was the Churchillian pronouncement of one American commentator. Inevitably, we misremember that first time and exaggerate and distort its excitement. As Vadim said, 'In the film she was undressed for no more than five minutes. Yet people insisted she was naked throughout.' I was one of the deceived. I remember her body in every cinemascopic detail; and yet seeing the film again, I realize she never once appears without some cloaking device (clothes, a strategically positioned towel, a sheet, clothes line, force field). In other words, the film only ever alludes to a state of nakedness: it says it without showing it. As in *Jaws*, where the predatory white shark is most fearsome when we see only the approaching fin and not when it rears its head above water, so in *And God Created Woman* BB's depravity is the product of omission and elision. The San Francisco Academy of Art voted her the 'Best Undressed Woman in the World', but we, the viewers, not Vadim, were personally responsible for undressing her.

To our eyes Brigitte was the theo-ontic in person, the beach, Being, the ocean and the open sky. She throbbed out pure presence. She was not just natural, she was Nature. She was not just free, she was Freedom. She was not just Beauty, she was Truth. She confirmed the existential adage that existence precedes essence. The miracle of it was that even though she had total liberty and transcended pathetic male attempts at control, even though she could not be chosen and she alone could choose, she nevertheless chose us. Or would choose us, given the opportunity. That was the irrevocable premise from which all our conclusions followed.

It was absurd, but then the phenomenon of falling in love was an exercise in absurdity. When Meursault shot the Arab on the beach, it was 'because of the sun', a certain vacillation in the equilibrium of the elements. When BB surrendered to Sachs after he dived sixty feet out of a helicopter into the sea, it was (she said in the *Daily Express*) because of 'the coincidence of things. His sudden arrival, my love for him, the sun of that day, the smells, all the things of that moment came together.' There was no logic to it: that was the logic.

We never had conversations with BB. She was beyond conversation. A glance, a gesture, a touch would suffice to notify us of her desire. Her English was bad, our French was worse, but her body was an international language, an erotic Esperanto in which we were as fluent as fish in the sea.

# 7

# D-Day 1944 and Easter 1968

Bardot apart, however, the feminine was defined by the necessity of persuasion. Ordinarily, the feminine deflected us from the linearity of action into the labyrinths of rhetoric. Perhaps if the girls we knew (but did not know) had held nothing back then we would never have been driven to St Tropez in pursuit of the elusive totality in the first place. The sixties was a time when a lot of women began to model themselves on Brigitte Bardot. 'I wish they all could be California girrrrls,' crooned the Beach Boys. But the Californians themselves were nothing other than clones, distant derivatives of BB. In Romford, Denise and Kathy were as close as we'd got to the archetype. Denise's blonde hair snaked loosely down her back while Kathy's was bobbed and bleached. Denise was shorter than the ideal, but even more prolifically endowed: her chest jutted out in front of her like the deck of an aircraft carrier and she had a pout like a surrealist sofa. 'She's a fuckin' walking right-angle!' Griffo exclaimed. Kathy was taller and more athletic, played badminton for the county and displayed a marked preference for older blokes with cars. 'You can't blame 'em, can you?' Griffo said. 'They get fed up with walking over Bedford's looking for a bush when they can hop in a motor and be taken over Hainault instead.' Denise was not so sporty, but if she'd run the 100 yards she could have breasted the tape from half-way.

According to Roger Vadim, he was seduced, aged sixteen, by a budding actress in a Normandy hayloft at precisely the moment the D-Day barrage opened up, so that 'not only the earth moved but the roof and the walls shook as well'. I had once got Susan

Wilkins down to her bra and the panties with little flowers on in the bushes adjacent to the deer paddock. A year later I saw her pushing a pram but I was reasonably confident that it had nothing to do with me. Sometimes you couldn't find an empty berth in Bedford's, half of Essex was there groping in the undergrowth, like salmon squirming upstream to spawn.

The first time Griffo and I went out with Denise and Kathy we took the train from Romford to Southend Victoria and back again. We didn't bother to get out the other end. It was raining and all we had was a return ticket to Gidea Park, the next station up the line, anyway. It was the kind of compartment that no longer exists and was only accessible by the outer door. We pulled down the blinds and unscrewed the bulb on the ceiling. But every time the train came to a halt, so did the girls. A straight-through and it might have been a different story, but it was an all-stations Sunday service, so short of doing a Buster Edwards and coshing her over the head to get my hands on the loot, I had to content myself with seeing Denise's shiny underwear, taut and full, flash past somewhere between Wick-ford and Rayleigh.

Thus it was that we skived off school for the day. 'Play hooky . . .' 'Have nooky!' we chanted. What we needed was a good clear run at them, a day without fear of interruption. It wasn't my idea we should use my house, but everyone else had at least one parent home, so they said. We met up at the corner of Highfield and Avalon, as guilty as thieves, and wormed our way along dusty alleyways before sneaking in through the back gate, silently lifting the latch so as not to alert snoopy Brenda on one side or snoozing Marcus the boxer-dog on the other. I was breaking into my own home.

'You're sure your Mum and Dad aren't going to come back?' Denise asked nervously as we plied them with Ty-Phoo and custard creams.

'What about your brothers?' Kathy said while we scrubbed the cups and plates and emptied the pot and wiped the prints.

'We hang about much longer,' protested Griffo, 'and they'll all be home for supper.'

We crept upstairs, treading softly on the carpet, Denise and I to my bedroom, Griffo and Kathy to my elder brother's next door. I had been careful to leave the curtains closed that morning so that there would be no clumsy semaphoring to the neighbours opposite. The sun had gone behind the house so the room lay in shadow. Denise and I lay on my bed and wrestled for a while. I got her skirt off, which she folded neatly and put on the foot of my twin brother's bed. But she still kept pulling down her jumper as if she were expecting another passenger to get on. Meanwhile, on the other side of the dividing wall, Kathy was deliquescing in Griffo's hot, sticky hands like vanilla icecream, as surely as Juliette had done in the arms of Jean-Louis Trintignant.

Denise had an uncle named Eric with a deep gruff voice who was dead. I knew this because he had paid a return visit from the afterlife on the occasion of a séance Denise had conducted at her house one night the week before, during which he had occupied her body and spoken with her voice, or at least her vocal chords, since it was the deep gruff voice of Uncle Eric that issued from her own disproportionate mouth. Four of us, Denise and I, my twin brother and Denise's younger cousin Linda, sat around a table in the light of a candle and linked hands and Denise, who had mystic powers, fell into a trance. It was a good pretext to hold hands with Denise, but I took the séance more seriously than mass on Sunday, even though I suspected there should by rights have been some ectoplasm.

'Is that you, Denise?' said the voice. 'This is your Uncle Eric.' He said he was doing okay considering and asked how her mum and dad were. But he couldn't get much of an answer out of her because she was in a trance at the time and anyway he was using her tongue. Then his monologue dipped into a more confessional vein. 'I'm sorry, Denise,' he repeated. 'I'm really sorry for what I did.' Denise couldn't explain, then or afterwards, even when old Eric had fled her body again.

On that Tuesday morning up in my bedroom she gave me the text of her entire life-story, not omitting distant relatives, like Scheherezade putting off her sentence. Eric, it transpired, wasn't distant enough. It wasn't just his spirit that had occupied Denise's body. Now it seemed as if you had to come straight out of Hades if you wanted to possess Denise. I didn't stand a chance, my path had been blocked by a dead man. All that abuse as a child had paralysed her, sexually, she said.

40

'I'm sorry, Andy,' she was saying, oddly echoing the ghost of Eric, 'I'm really sorry.'

'That's all right,' I sympathized, taking the opportunity to sneak my hands up her jumper again.

'I may not always be this way, you know,' Denise said.

'No?' I said, brightening.

'It's just a matter of time.'

'Any idea how long exactly?'

'It's unpredictable. It could be weeks or days . . .'

Erection.

'. . . or it could be *years*.'

Detumescence.

'I need lots of affection to exorcize the ghost.'

She kept on talking but I wasn't really listening and anyway it all came down to the same thing, that those stupendous breasts of hers that seemed almost to be reaching out and embracing you and welcoming you in were as inaccessible as the hereafter.

It must have been around noon when I heard a car pull up outside the house and I leapt to the window, tweaking the curtain aside, glad of an excuse to get up from the rack. It was my father's black Hillman Humber, black as a Black Maria. I bundled Denise into the room with Griffo and Kathy, throwing her skirt in after her and praying the glutton wouldn't have her for seconds. Kathy's cream jumper lay discarded on the floor, and she had her bra off (Exhibit A: compact but accessible), but I established beyond reasonable doubt that the pleated skirt remained hooked at the waist. 'My Dad's back!' I yelled, slamming the door shut again. 'Keep quiet and don't move, for God's sake.'

'We're fucked if he comes upstairs,' Griffo said.

I was stuffing my shirt down my trousers and straightening my hair as the front door opened. I popped my head round the banisters. 'Hello, Dad.' I had no difficulty sounding as sick as I was supposed to be.

'Hello, son. You feeling better?'

'Coming round. You're home early.'

'Left some papers behind,' he said. 'Meeting.'

Denise's lips were tattooed all over my face, and the sound of breath being held was blasting out of my big brother's bedroom as Slipper of the Yard climbed the stairs. 'Now where did your

41

mother put . . .? Why does she always have to . . . Oh, right, got 'em. Got to run, I'm late, bye son.'

'Jesus, Holy Mary, God the Father, thank you, thank you, thank you.' Griffo was crossing himself. 'You bastard, Andy.'

We staggered out of the back door and took deep breaths in the garden, like Lloyd Bridges spluttering up to the surface in *Sea Quest* after having had his air-pipe severed by some particularly unscrupulous villains. Marcus was sniffing at the fence but I was beyond worrying about the neighbours.

'How'd you get on?' I said.

'Got a bit of tit. God, she's got a lovely pair on her. You?'

A familiar litany, with its pattern of versicles and responses. Some inspiration made us think of swapping partners there and then. Wife-swapping was rife in the Home Counties: we read about it in magazines and composed answers to ads seeking 'uninhibited and fun-loving couples'. So why not Denise and Kathy? Griffo fancied Denise and I fancied Kathy and therefore, we assumed, vice-versa. It was up to me to put the proposal. 'Tell her I'll join her coven if she'll let me feel her tits,' said Griffo.

'Ever thought about swapping partners?' I said, opting for the oblique approach. They stared. 'Just for the afternoon, like. As an experiment, I mean.'

Tears sprang to Denise's eyes. Kathy laid into us. 'You bloody boys, you're all the bloody same, all you want to do is fuck us and you don't give a shit who. We could put a sack over our heads and you wouldn't notice the difference.'

Her diatribe had us back-pedalling so fast that it was to be a full year before I would get Kathy on my lap while she leafed fervently through a mail-order catalogue.

# 8

## 20 December and 30 December 1952

SEE! Roman Legions! SEE! Nero's Harem! SEE!
Dreaded slave galleys! SEE! Roman orgies! SEE! Bardot
bathe in milk!
Publicity poster for *Mio figlio Nerone* (Nero's Mistress/Nero's Weekend)

If only they had seen the movie. Denise and Kathy didn't realize
that BB had invented a new persona for women: the female Don
Juan with polyandrous desires and the balls to satisfy them. In
film after film Bardot unholsters a loaded phallic symbol, cocks
and fires it, for no apparent aesthetic reason beyond her
transexual machismo. That was what we needed above all: a
girl who would come up to us and say, 'Fuck me!' It sometimes
seemed as if the only sex in Essex was in the second syllable.

Anyone born in Warsaw, brought up in Alexandria, then
transposed to Cannes and Paris after the sudden death of his
father, who slumped face forwards into a bowl of coffee at the
breakfast table, would automatically have a head-start. These
were the insuperable advantages of Roger Vadim, the man whose
shoes most men in the Western world would have sold their souls
to step into. Roger Vladimir Plemiannikoff, handsome son of a
concupiscent White Russian diplomat and collateral descendant
of Genghis Khan, kidnapped by Turks as a six-year-old and now
one of the rootless post-World War Two Left Bank crowd, on
nodding terms with Jean Cocteau, André Gide and Colette. Gide
compared him to Lafcadio in *The Vatican Cellars*, the man who
could get away with any *acte gratuit*. 'And Vadim Created
Bardot', that was the catchphrase. According to Simone de
Beauvoir a woman is not born but made, and it was Vadim who
made Bardot, according to Vadim, converting or corrupting her,
turning her from a shy, goofy, bourgeois virgin into an

uninhibited extrovert and exhibitionist and sex-maniac – a Dr Frankenstein figure who had put her together out of spare-part male fantasies and then lost control of his monster. Or was he simply the midwife, spectating appreciatively as she evolved and metamorphosed before his eyes?

There was a time, it was said, when Brigitte was ugly. The name by which she was christened invoked a Celtic fire-goddess; perhaps the alliteration was suggested by Simone Simon. But she soon acquired astigmatism, wire-framed spectacles and braces on her buck teeth. And the reflection in the mirror persisted in her own eyes. Pilou, as Brigitte called her father, Louis Bardot, was chairman and managing director of Bardot & Cie, the largest liquid oxygen manufacturer in France and an amateur poet who, it was believed, had won a prize from the French Academy for an early volume. He it was who encouraged her impersonations of Charlie Chaplin and shot the original moving pictures of her on a cine camera.

She studied ballet in Paris under Boris Kniazeff, spent her summers at Biarritz, and wintered in Méribel. She modelled her mother's millinery to the strains of *Swan Lake*, but the young Brigitte first appeared to the general public in the Junior Miss pages of *Jardin des modes*, with neatly parted hair, a toothy grin, and a crocheted top. She was aged fourteen and already she was 34–20–34, but not yet blonde. Within a few months she had made the transition to the front cover of *Elle* with the same smile in a dress with a bow in front, cinched at the waist, and identified only by her initials on the insistence of her protective mother, Anne-Marie, who naively supposed that 'BB' would safeguard her anonymity. Marc Allégret, producer of *Les Lauriers sont coupés*, Vadim's first (unfilmed) script, rejected her at her screen-test on account of her laugh and her teeth. But Vadim himself, who tore the cover off the May 1949 number of *Elle*, stuck by her and his instincts, and by the time Castro was overthrowing the ancien régime in Havana, BB had been unveiled as a one-woman sexual revolution.

'He revealed me to myself,' said BB. But, as Sartre would say, there was no essence of BB that either preceded or succeeded *And God Created Woman*, no soul of BB to be taken out and inspected. She was nothing other than her actions. And that included her on-screen persona. She was an unbroken continuum between what happened in front of and behind the camera. Vadim had to twist her arm to accept Trintignant as her screen lover, but once the decision was taken it was inevitable that she should continue to consort with him off-screen too. Vadim seemed to give his blessing to the union. There was a rumour, which we willingly believed, that the love scenes were not faked, that when Vadim yelled 'Cut!' only the cameras stopped and BB and Jean-Lou kept right on rolling. 'I love everything about her,' Trintignant is reported to have said, 'except that she is Brigitte Bardot.' Detained by national service, Trintignant would quickly be displaced by Sacha Distel, originally recruited to teach Bardot the rudiments of the guitar. No man dared leave BB alone in bed for too long. The space next to her was a vacuum that her nature abhorred.

Vadim, that most enviable of men, now cuts a slightly tragic or comic figure. He married Brigitte at the Notre Dame de Grace in Passy on 20 December 1952. Ten days after their union, on the 30th, I was born in East Ham Hospital. Vadim advertised his wife as the unattainable dream of all married men and she thereby became unattainable for her own husband. It is some consolation to those of us who never married her that she seems to have driven her husbands to distraction. A kind of Schadenfreude runs through me when I read Vadim's own autobiographical account – self-glorifying though it is – of his conquests in *Bardot, Deneuve, Fonda*. Perhaps only Rod Stewart (who began his career, like John Lennon, fixating on Bardot) can claim to have bedded so many tall, blonde, similar women. And yet, as was my fate in the case of Denise, who belonged to Uncle Eric, Vadim could not be said to have possessed Bardot. He was almost as much a voyeur of his own wife as we were. He could only really enjoy her from the other side of a camera, or gazing through the eyes of others.

The opening of his memoirs recalls an episode from 12 May 1953, when two thousand American sailors on board the aircraft carrier *Enterprise* (others claim it was the *Midway*, but Vadim, perhaps warped by *Star Trek*, boldly prefers the name of the Federation flagship) anchored in the bay at Cannes, saw BB for the first time. She was a virtually unknown starlet with a CV which included the minor comedy *Le Trou normand* (translated as *Crazy for Love* and, bafflingly, *Ti Ta To*) and worked her ticket to the Festival on the back of *Act of Love*, a Franco-American production starring Kirk Douglas and Dany Robin. Until then the marines had been exposed only to Bob Hope's entertainment-for-the-troops package. BB suddenly summarized everything they had gone to sea to see. It was like Columbus discovering the New World.

First they saw her long tresses floating on the surface of the water; then her face, streaming with drops of water, glistening in the sun like so many diamonds. Her innocent, sensual mouth and perfect oval eyes, her delicate nose, her cheeks as round as a child's, were made for pleasure and laughter. Two hands with aristocratic wrists gripped the edge of the Chris-Craft and the apparition hoisted herself on board; a delicate neck, a thin waist that a man could encircle with two hands; a round, provocative and tender derrière that would have been the envy of Adonis and Aphrodite; perfectly curved hips, long, firm thighs, charming ankles, and the arched feet of a dancer. A little bikini, a shadow rather than a garment, hid nothing of this sensual, glorious body.

So, too, it must have been that Vadim more truly had knowledge of his own wife when she gave herself to Trintignant. He craved the admiration of other men and their desire for BB. It was not that he lost her, first to her co-star and then, in marriage to her second husband, Jacques Charrier, but that he only gained her at the very moment he was losing her and she became the property of all and of none. He loved her most on celluloid, on billboards and in the eyes and arms of others. The irony is that even as we were fantasizing about being Vadim, he was fantasizing about being us.

46

# 9

## May 1968

BARDOT: Qu'est-ce que vous êtes venu faire ici?
CHARRIER: Rejoindre le Général de Gaulle.
BARDOT: Qui c'est celui-là?
CHARRIER: C'est celui qui distribue les billets pour le
retour en France.
BARDOT: Voilà l'homme que je cherchais!

*Babette s'en va-t-en guerre*

(BARDOT: What have you come to do here?
CHARRIER: To join up with General de Gaulle.
BARDOT: Who is he?
CHARRIER: He is the one who is handing out return
tickets to France.
BARDOT: Why, that's just the man I was looking for!

*Babette Goes to War*)

'It is very possible that Britain's own evolution, and the evolution of the universe, might bring the English towards the Continent, whatever delays this achievement might demand.' This was General de Gaulle's elaborate way of giving us the cold shoulder in January 1963. But Griffo and I weren't about to let the President of France or an uncooperative universe stand in our way.

In sixties newspapers, radio and television, the topos France boiled down to two essential stories. One was about Brigitte Bardot; the other was about General de Gaulle. They were presented as antithetical, but in truth they were complementary, almost mirror-images of one another, and they still run concurrently on the front page of my memory.

In one the ageing president, still wearing military uniform some twenty years after the war officially ceased, is saying (in banner headlines an inch high) 'NON!' (with small variations such as 'NON! NON! NON!') to our entry into the then Common Market. There is an accompanying cartoon in which Mr Macmillan (and later Harold Wilson) appears as a pink-cheeked and sighing suitor, while de Gaulle is a whiskery *femme fatale* in fishnet tights who haughtily rejects our advances (alternatively, it would be a replay of Waterloo with de Gaulle/Napoleon winning, Blücher/Adenauer going over to the French, and Macmillan/Wellington crushed and defeated).

In the other, which provided a kind of compensation, Brigitte Bardot, usually wearing the bare minimum, is saying 'OUI!' to a succession of lovers (Mike Sarne, Gunther Sachs, Andy Martin, Steve Griffin). The soldier is old, ugly and vertical; the film-star is young, beautiful and horizontal. The contrast could hardly be more marked. He belongs to Paris and the Elysée Palace and Colombey-les-Deux-Eglises; she is inseparable from the south, the sun, the sand. He embodies the empire of the past; she the *nouveau monde amoureux* of the future. He is the father of the nation; she refuses to be a mother.

It was as if GG and BB were at war. In 1961 Bardot received a letter demanding a contribution of 50 million old francs towards the OAS campaign to assassinate de Gaulle and threatening to blow up La Madrague for non-compliance; it turned out to come from a conman buying himself a hotel in Switzerland, but the idea of BB in league with the 'Secret Army' was not implausible (hence she had to be seen to outgeneral the General in a public offensive at the Billancourt film studios: 'I swear that I will fight to the death against Fascism'). When she married Sachs on Bastille Day in 1967, de Gaulle was furious with her for once again stealing the limelight.

But there were affinities between these antagonists. It seems on the face of it unlikely that anyone should have confused the two. But if not then why should Bardot's lawyer have been moved to announce to the world in 1965: 'My client is not General de Gaulle: she has not made a gift of her person to the nation.' Her second husband, Jacques Charrier, her co-star in *Babette s'en va-t-en guerre* (1959), resented precisely that she had not made a gift of herself to him: 'You can't have for yourself what belongs to the whole of the country, whether it is Brigitte Bardot or Camembert cheese.'

After visiting the set and watching his wife make love to four different men – auditioning for Clouzot's *La Vérité* – Charrier demanded she quit there and then. Then he took to brawling with Sami Frey, her next co-star and presumed lover, lying in wait and pouncing as they stepped out of the car. Perhaps impregnating her, forcing her to be a bad mother, was a kind of revenge. He suffered breakdowns and twice attempted suicide. Questions were asked in the National Assembly. 'What measures is the government proposing to take to ensure that all recruits are treated equally even when they come from the arms of a great actress?' The commanding officer of his barracks at Epinal, where he had been posted to a signals unit, banned all BB pin-ups on the grounds that the constant sight of pictures of his wife tacked on walls and lockers had compounded Charrier's despair. But the blank walls and bare lockers spoke eloquently to him of her absence. In the end he had to be discharged from the army for battle fatigue on the home front: *inapte à servir* was the shameful verdict on this son of a soldier. It was a symbolic defeat for de Gaulle.

General de Gaulle was the Frenchman who had evicted the invader and liberated France from Nazi oppression. Bardot, raised in Paris under the Occupation and finding in the lovers who occupied her shelter against the terrors of the night, stood for another liberation, which impinged on us directly: this time sexual, from centuries, from millennia, of repression. In a sense, BB was the natural successor to de Gaulle. In *Babette s'en va-t-en guerre*, she turns soldier to save England from a German invasion by seducing the Nazi High Command. It was inevitable that she should be the model for a new bust of Marianne, the symbol of the Republic which adorns town halls throughout France, presiding over every marriage in the country.

Griffo and I saw all women through BB-tinted glasses. Only when we took them off did we discover we'd been making advances to General de Gaulle. Messrs Macmillan and Heath, Wilson and Brown, were beating at the door to get into the Common Market when all we wanted was to get into Bardot. 'Free trade' we understood as code for free love. Meanwhile the anti-marketeers, like Victorian chaperones, conspired with the General to keep us chastely in our separate beds.

'Do you realize,' Griffo said to me as we kicked a ball about in his back garden, 'there are some people who go through their entire lives without ever getting their oats? Nuns, for example. To get closer to God.'

I flicked the ball off toes, knee and head for a count of ten, and then coiled it into the air off my heel.

'You think there could be something in it?' he pondered, the ball poised in the crook of his neck. 'Look at footballers. They're not allowed to have it away on a Friday night, are they, so they're still hungry for the big match. One shag and you're shagged. Fuck and you're fucked.' He whiplashed the ball into the air.

'On that basis we should both be playing like bloody Pele,' I said, booting at the ball bitterly and volleying it over the fence. The terrible truth was that at age fifteen we had hit our peak, football-wise, and were already on the slide. We were not yet fourteen when we won the World Cup, it was hard to recapture the high of the Hurst hat-trick. In lieu of playing for England, we took up BB as our personal goal.

There were unmistakable signs of union between England and France, beyond the Anglo-French production of *Two Weeks in September*. We had been building Concorde together since November 1962. Admittedly, there had been hitches. Unlike any other plane, the nose section rose and fell; also unlike any other plane, it couldn't actually take off. The fuselage was as slim as a pencil; but where would the passengers fit? But the main problem was the quarrel over how to spell the name. And in the second half of the sixties, real progress was achieved when we at last agreed to stick a French 'e' on the end of 'concord'. Concorde became officially feminine.

And then there was Supravyl. We never actually saw any Supravyl, but a half-page advertisement headed 'Vive la différence!' in the *Daily Mail* of 7 September 1966 ('Brigitte Bardot spent yesterday, the first day of filming in Scotland, trying to keep warm'), convinced us that everything was falling into place. 'It was pretty smart of the French to think up Supravyl,' I quoted.

'What the hell is Supravyl?' Griffo said.

'It's an absolutely unique fabric,' I replied, 'the only predominantly wool jersey-knit fabric that is as *carefree* as a synthetic.

You're wondering why is Supravyl so different?'

'OK, why is Supravyl so different?'

'I'll tell you. Supravyl is made in England from natural wool and RHOVYL, the sensational synthetic fibre that has more advantages that any other known. It won't sag or wrinkle, stays in shape, is machine washable, dries fast, doesn't matt, shrink or fade. But you probably won't care, because it looks and feels so good.'

The future stitched together England and France, the natural and the synthetic, in a seamless fabric that would not sag or wrinkle, shrink or fade. Meanwhile, we did what we could to change our luck. There were rituals to perform. As we left the house to go into town Griffo would pause at the dusty print of the Madonna in the hallway. Deftly removing the stopper from the phial, he splashed Brut behind his left ear, and then dabbed a spot of holy water from the porcelain font behind the right. Following the logic of the Pascalian wager, that you have nothing to lose by believing and everything to gain, I emulated his moves. Looking back on it now, I can see there was a fundamental fallacy in seeking a sexual panacea from the Virgin Mary.

Having shrewdly failed the 11-plus Griffo had elected to go to Chase Cross secondary modern, where roughly a million girls were in love with him. Lucky devil, going to a mixed school, I brooded one grudgy, needling Saturday in Stones, still strapped into my royal blue Royal Liberty blazer after a school match.

'It's not mixed,' he protested, 'it's separate. Boys up one end, girls up the other.'

For a moment I wasn't so hard done-by. The world seemed a better and kinder place.

'There's no fraternizing, only before school and after, and break-times. You have to hop over the fence into Bedford's.'

That wasn't enough for his sweethearts. They got their little brothers to slip swooning declarations daubed with arrowed hearts into his desk. There were constraints, though, which evened things out between us. Girls rang him up all the time, but if his mother, who wanted him to have an education, took the call, she would yell down the phone, 'Leave my Steven alone.' 'I don't want him becoming a stoopid navvy like his father,' she explained to his teachers.

51

But Ma Griffin was not in the same league as the Parrish brothers, who lived in King's Hill where all the hard cases lived. It was a classic Racinian triangle: Dave Parrish adored Pat Smith who adored Griffo: Griffo was divided between deflowering Pat Smith and staying alive. Parrish was a runt and Griffo had the beating of him. But he was a runt with a litter of big brothers and every time Griffo got him down they were queuing up to kick his head in. One year at Romford Carnival in Raphael's Park, amid the floats and pearly queens, about ninety of the Parrishes caught him having a good time with Pat Smith and he ran off and crawled under a Vauxhall Zodiac whence he could see the steel toe-caps of the Parrishes milling on all sides and hear his own doom foretold in gruesome detail: 'I'll get that fuckin' Griffin if it's the last thing I fuckin' do. I'm going to chop his dick off and stuff it down his gob.'

'The Carnival is a very tense time,' he told me as he put himself on the couch in Stones, constructing a leaning tower out of Tate & Lyle sugar cubes and perching the salt cellar on top.

'I'll have to stop going to confession. The father'll be getting pissed off with the old lustful thoughts all the time. Last week he asked whether I had had carnal knowledge of a woman. He wants something he can get his teeth into, he's practically begging me to get on with it.'

When he took me along to mass after football one Sunday, Griffo explained the concept of original sin to me. 'It's built into us, like plumbing or wiring. You can put up walls and slap paint on, but it's still there, humming away. Thank God.' He was a builder's son and he saw God as the Builder and original sin as the solid foundation, a cast-iron guarantee of a good time to come.

Catholics believed things, odd things, almost anything, the odder the better. Papal infallibility, the Holy Trinity, the rhythm method, resonant phrases whose meaning was a mystery to me. Griffo reckoned he had heard the soul departing from the body of a dead man. It was like a puff of smoke or the rustling of trees. Theologically, I should never have been playing for the Corpus Christi Catholic Boys XI. I was C of E and didn't have to believe a thing: no sin, no hell, no heaven, thank you very much, just carols at Christmas and chocolate eggs at Easter and a symbolic reading of the Book of Genesis. But the Catholics were missing a left-winger, so I was in.

As with beliefs, so too with clothes: Griffo had more of them and more interesting ones. I remember the first time I ever saw him in anything other than football kit. He was wearing a pair of C&A tweed trousers with an outsize houndstooth check and a spearmint ribbed sleeveless cardigan. From then on, everything he wore defined style for me, was the embodiment of the Beautiful: Fred Perrys, flares and vents, Millett's flying jackets, calf-high riding boots, the bespoke dark-brown sheepskin from Leroy Furs, Sergeant Pepper khaki and epaulettes. He eschewed stereotypes, the extreme manifestations of mod and rocker, skinhead and hippy. You wouldn't catch him riding a Lambretta in a Parka with a fur-trimmed hood, its back inscribed with benedictions of The Who, or sporting red clip-on braces over a blue Ben Sherman button-down, any more than you would in full greaser regalia of leathers and Castrol 20/50. He was a trend-setter who ran free of the herd and was hard to keep pace with. It was like Mike Sarne trying to live up to Gunther Sachs, who, we noted, at his wedding, wore a black mohair blazer, white flannel trousers, white silk shirt open to the waist (with a dense hairy décolletage we dared not even dream of) and Gucci loafers (and this was the key) without socks. As Glenys Roberts reverentially records in her book, *Bardot: A Personal Biography*, that subtle sartorial omission 'would become a talking point to be emulated by everyone in those circles to this day'.

One Easter, when I went to Paris with my school, they sent out pages of precautionary instructions to my parents, in case I too should neglect to wear socks. The list of do's and don't's ran to a small book: all I remember was that *Suit (grey)* figured in the list of requisites. I was fourteen and saw the two-piecer as my passport to maturity. I tried to steer my mother into Brent and Collins, a branch of Take-Six (with its headquarters in Carnaby Street), where Griffo and I spent Saturdays when we weren't in Stones and I had my eye on a double-breasted pinstripe, Chicago gangster-style, with a fedora to top it off. But she fixed on Bodgers instead, the men's outfitters with a 'youth' department, and interpreted that parenthesis over-literally. The (dark grey) worsted two-button I came out with was my most carbuncular adolescent embarrassment, a sure-fire giveaway of the juvenile, a leaden liability it took me only a year or two to grow out of and a quarter of a century to live down. It didn't even have a vent, an incommensurable catastrophe when your manhood was measured, like Chinese pigtails, by the length of your centre vent. Ten inches was the ideal, even though I would have settled for eight, but there was a certified case of a fifteen-incher that went nearly up to the shoulders. The double vent was unorthodox. But no vent at all was anathema.

I was almost spared that twenty-five-year blush. When Phil Dines, the first boy I ever heard to utter the word 'clitoris' and look like he knew whereof he spoke and universally regarded as the snappiest dresser in school, once asked if he could borrow the grey worsted for a day, I felt an unaccustomed surge of pride. Perhaps it was a forgotten classic about to make a comeback. Fashion – prickly, unpredictable, flighty fashion – had turned a corner and finally come round to my mother's *Weltanschauung*.

'How'd you get on with the whistle, Phil?' I asked as he handed it back wrapped up in a brown paper bag.

'Fine,' he said. 'I wouldn't have asked only I couldn't find anything in my wardrobe sombre enough for a funeral.'

That was the kiss of death, the last rites for me and my suit. It wasn't a suit but a coffin, and I was the corpse. I had to get rid of the bugger at all costs. I fantasized about returning home and telling my mother how I'd been trapped in a blazing inferno and that lovely suit she'd bought me, you know the grey one, the worsted, it was burned right off my back; alternatively, I would be the victim of a knife-attack and it would be slashed to shreds. But I could never work out how to come out of it personally unscathed.

Griffo alone did not despise the suit and always claimed it was acceptable clobber. There was a thin vein of solidarity in his attitude, but it was encased within the shrewd consciousness of the massive edge it gave him. 'You wearing the Bodger tonight?' he would ask, knowing all along it would sink me like cement. If you were going to the Ilford Palais the suit was *de rigueur*, even on a Saturday afternoon, if you wanted to pull a bird; at the Uppercut (one of boxer Billy Walker's clubs where The Four Tops and Stevie Wonder played) the bouncers wouldn't let you past the door without one.

Griffo, who would not be seen dead in grey worsted himself, had acquired a shimmery mohair two-piece with high lapels, in chocolate brown, that he liked to wear with all three buttons done up, just as Jean-Louis Trintignant had done in *And God Created Woman* before Juliette unbuttoned it for him. Once, on South Street, on a Sunday afternoon, as we swaggered towards the station, suited up and carefully coiffeured, silk handkerchiefs blossoming from breast pockets, we passed a couple of toe-capped skinheads going the other way and I heard one of them say appraisingly, 'Did you book the chocolate brown mohair?' 'Yeah,' sighed his mate. 'But what about that fucking stupid grey one!'

It wasn't until much later, too late, that I finally covered my shame with a green mohair three-button. Plain mohair, not the tonik weave that gave off a metallic fluorescence and was the characteristic complexion of the upper echelons of the smart set. I did have a pair of brown tonik trousers made up at Burtons, high-waisted, with a key pocket, which glinted with red and black pixels. But by then Griffo had shifted the paradigm with a loose oatmeal bespoke herringbone with patch pockets, which he inherited from his elder brother John.

With notable exceptions such as the frock jacket and the shoes with hooks instead of eyelets, my parents approved of this gear. They thought suits and ties and silk hankies and short hair (but not skinhead) were 'smart'. There was nothing for it but to switch to long hair, bell bottoms and collarless shirts dyed purple or pink.

Griffo's hair grew long and thick and unregulated and he would have sprouted muttonchop sideburns if he could. My headmaster, a specialist in geometry, stipulated that hair should touch neither collar nor ears, as if they were Euclidean parallel lines that should only meet at infinity. One day he sent me out to the local barbers to get mine cut down to size. I persuaded the barber to go easy on the clippers and plaster everything back with gel, but J. P. Coles (MA, Cantab.) was wise to that trick and combed it all out and ordered me back for a total crop on pain of caning and suspension. A group of hardcore radical fifth-formers barricaded themselves into a small top-floor classroom one Friday, resolved to grow our hair long or die, but the revolt fizzled out when we paused to consider the time it would take to make any perceptible difference. We had been impressed by the newspaper photograph of a kidnapped Italian businessman who after three or four days in a Red Brigade hideout already looked shaggy and grizzled. But there wasn't a hope in hell of any of us starting to look unshaven in much under a year or two.

My parents rightly concluded I was going about collecting bad influences like stamps with precious defects and they homed in on Griffo as the Penny Black in my album. 'Are you going out with that boy Griffin again?' was their regular refrain. 'Can't you find someone nicer?' But the axe didn't actually fall until one Sunday in May.

We caught the train from Romford to Ilford and turned out of the station towards Valentine's Park, stripped down to our grandpa vests, bought second-hand with age-old sweat stains, then boiled and dyed salmon pink and sunburst yellow. But we hadn't gone more than twenty yards when the two most beautiful girls we had ever seen for the last five minutes went by us in the opposite direction. We swivelled round and followed them. One was tall and dark, the other small and fair. They drifted along the high street, gazing in shop windows. So we drifted and paused and gazed too, mainly at them. We gave them the eye. The thing about giving someone the eye is you can never exactly tell when they look at you whether they're giving you the eye back again or just looking at you and wishing you'd stop looking at them. And while we were sizing up a windowful of Hoovers and Hotpoints, they suddenly vanished. We put on a burst of speed. But we had lost them. We ducked into the shadows of an arcade to regroup. 'Where the fuckin' 'ell did they go?' groaned Griffo.

The answer, the two answers, were standing there, looking at us, in the arcade, where they had taken refuge. 'You seem to have been avoiding us,' I challenged them. Well, it worked for Gunther. But he probably said it in French.

Griffo was the acknowledged master of chat, the suave exponent of winning one-liners. I was all right so long as I could perfect my lines in the bath or during botched afternoons of woodwork (my dovetailed joints never dovetailed, my magazine rack and my milk dial ended up as a milk rack and a magazine dial) before they had to be aired in public. But where I needed to think about what I was doing before I did it, nailing my words together with a dictionary and a grammar, Griffo was a natural, a genius of spontaneity, an improviser who never thought about what he was doing and did it with complete conviction even when he went wrong. So why was it I always had to stick my head up over the trench first, just asking to get it shot off? I was cannon fodder, he was the general bringing up the rear and claiming victory.

'Here, were you following us?' the tall one said.

We admitted we were but promised we'd stop if they'd come over to Valentine's with us. They looked at one another in resignation, linked arms and came quietly. They were window-dressers at C&A. The short one was called Chrissie. That night we saw an off-shoot of The Small Faces fronted by Steve Marriott playing at the Willow dance hall off Mawney Road. Chrissie was crazy about Steve Marriott. In the porch of a nearby tobacconist she ground up against me with her groin till my fly was ready to pop and we made a date with them in Valentine's for the following Saturday and they didn't turn up and we never saw them again.

We missed the last bus and we had to hoof it and it was well into Monday morning when I finally made it home. My mother, who had been waiting up, hit the roof. 'What time do you think this is? Another five minutes and I would have phoned the police. And what about your O-levels? Do you ever stop to think about that?' She choked like she had a fishbone stuck in her throat and focused her eyes on a spot a couple of inches below my chin. That was when it came over me in a sickly rush that I had forgotten to remove the white waiter's jacket and the necklace of flowers. In the Willow they were a smash hit, but back in Highfield Road, they bombed.

'What's all this nonsense you've got on? Plastic flowers round your neck? I expect you've been smoking pot as well. Get it off and never let me see you wearing it again.'

Then she turned nasty, aggravated by my air of philosophical resignation, which seemed to confirm the drugs hypothesis. 'It's all this boy Griffin's fault, isn't it?'

By then even my father had got up to chime in. 'That's the last time I want you hanging about with that Griffin. The last time, do you hear?'

# 10

# May 1968 Continued

Le cinéma, disait André Bazin, substitue à notre regard un
monde qui s'accorde à nos désirs. *Le Mépris* est l'histoire de
ce monde.

*Le Mépris*

(Cinema, André Bazin said, substitutes for our gaze a
world which is in accordance with our desires.
*Contempt* is the history of this world.

*Contempt*)

Back in 1968, when Griffo and I were discussing Simone de
Beauvoir's essay, 'Brigitte Bardot and the Lolita Syndrome', it
occurred to us that she had misread the significance of BB . . .

I wish I could begin a sentence that way. André Gide, with his
battalions of immensely well-read schoolboys, might have done.
It is not impossible that we, aged fifteen, could have encountered
that seminal article. Simone de Beauvoir, then aged fifty-one,
published it in the August 1959 number of *Esquire*. *Esquire* was
the kind of magazine we came across lying around the barber
shops we frequented, at Jeff and Phil's for example, although the
chances of us reading Beauvoir's encomium would have been
higher had it come out a few years later in *Playboy* or *Knave* or
*Penthouse*. I like to imagine that Griffo would have said, 'Hey,
Andy, take a butcher's at this, will you,' and handed me the
relevant much thumbed and contemplated page, and I would
have said, 'Mmm, but have you noticed the perspicacious essay
by Simone de Beauvoir overleaf . . .?'

According to Beauvoir, the secret of BB's attraction is that she
is a Lolita-type – a 'nymphet', as immortalized by Nabokov, a
child-woman. Perhaps this might have been plausible a few years

before: in her first film she is only eighteen and could have passed for a rebellious pubescent. But by 1959 Beauvoir's is already a dubious theory. Bardot is twenty-five; Nabokov's heroine is only twelve. Perhaps when you're over fifty, your perspective contracts and you can no longer tell the difference between twenty-five and fifteen; whereas we, on the other hand, could pinpoint ages, like Professor Higgins locating streets or even houses, to within a month or weeks (Griffo was a month older than me, with perceptibly fewer freckles and more whiskers, and it was like seeing my future) and construed anyone more than one year older than us as fully formed. Beauvoir justifies herself by remarking that 'If we wish to understand what BB represents, it is useless to make the acquaintance of the young woman named Brigitte Bardot.' The myth and the individual who happens to represent it must be scrupulously distinguished. True, Bardot still had big baby-brown eyes and a connotation of childishness and none of her roles ever stipulates an iota of maturity, responsibility, moderation. *BB, Bébé*: the name fitted Beauvoir's thesis perfectly.

Beauvoir goes so far as to speak of BB and Audrey Hepburn in the same breath, as inventors of the 'erotic *garçon manqué*'. In *Viva Maria!* (1965), Bardot briefly passes herself off as a more voluptuous Mowgli, blonde hair piled up under a cap, cheeks scrubbed with dirt, before deflowering into hourglass womanhood. But Beauvoir's analysis makes more sense in moral than physical terms: BB has the psychological disposition of a teenager; she is innocent as a child, beyond good and evil, devoid of bad faith, a model of existentialist authenticity.

Beauvoir begins her essay by recalling that, at a studio showing of a programme in which BB plays the guitar and dances, women in the audience were stoutly unimpressed by her beauty: 'She's not even pretty,' they muttered. 'She has the face of a housemaid.' Even the men were contemptuous. 'Only two or three of us, among thirty or so spectators, thought her charming. Then she did an excellent classical dance number. "She *can* dance," the others admitted grudgingly. Once again I was able to observe that Brigitte Bardot was disliked in her own country.' Except among the most avant-garde intelligentsia, BB was (and still is) scorned in Paris, while she had become the idol of

American youth. Shunned on the Champs-Elysées, *Et Dieu créa la femme* made a fortune in the States: four million dollars, the equivalent then of 2,500 Dauphine cars. Hence Beauvoir's quip that 'BB is now regarded as a more valuable export than Renault automobiles.' She may have sunk the morals of a nation, but at least she had saved the balance of payments. Beauvoir's theory is that BB is young, and so too is the States, while France is pathologically old in its outlook and customs. BB's destiny was single-handedly to engineer a renaissance.

Many years later, Beauvoir would say that this essay was one of her favourites among her own works. It's hard to resist the suspicion that there is a certain sentimental attachment involved. Beauvoir was, beyond dispute, a beautiful woman herself, who had many liaisons. Did she in some way identify with BB? Was Beauvoir the BB of the intellectual left? The idea is appealing. Beauvoir wrote *The Second Sex*, on the unfreedom of women, a corrective to the statement of universal and unfettered liberty (sicklied o'er with viscosity and vomiting) in Sartre's *Being and Nothingness*, at the end of the forties. Woman has been the victim of a patriarchal conspiracy, runs the argument, but has been an accomplice in her own repression. What is needed as a preliminary to wide-ranging renovation is a change of attitude: a re-affirmation of freedom.

Then, out of the grey uniformity of the fifties, and heralding the hallucinatory transcendentalism of the sixties, comes BB, almost like the answer to Beauvoir's prayers. BB was a female fantasy too, the prototypical feminist of the decades to come. She could acquire men, use them and discard them just as men had done to women for millennia. She got through men like a monkey with a bunch of bananas.

PAUL: Yesterday you still loved me?
CAMILLE: Yes, very much. Today it's over.
PAUL: Is there a reason?
CAMILLE: Yes, of course.
PAUL: What is it?
CAMILLE: I don't know. All I know is that I no longer love you.

(*Le Mépris*)

BB was sexual egalitarianism in action. Historically, her legacy may be seen to underwrite a caricature of carnal capitalism, the athletic accumulation of orgasms, the subordination of the feminine to a crude masculine stereotype; but at the end of the fifties, how could Beauvoir not see her as a redeeming symbol of herself and her own sexual and political imperatives?

And yet Beauvoir never compared herself to other women, only to another man. It has been held against her that she writes about women as if she were not one. As Deirdre Bair affirms in her biography, 'Beauvoir chose to interpret her status in the world in terms of her relationship with Sartre.' She and Sartre met at the Ecole Normale Supérieure while they were both studying for their Agrégation in philosophy, and they remained together for the next fifty years. Each – and especially Sartre – pursued other affairs, but they always returned to one another. They never married, and despised marriage as yet another capitalist con-trick, but each became, in Charles Fourier's poignant word, the other's *pivotal(e)*. Sartre wrote regularly to the Beaver, reporting the details of his latest conquests. And then they would see each other and talk about Descartes or Spinoza or Marx, and it would be like the first time all over again. It was as if Sartre was fixed in the Beaver's perception as a philosophy student at the Ecole. Until the moment of his death, he never grew old in her eyes. Sartre, too, was a myth, like BB; perhaps all people are. When Beauvoir was writing about Bardot's sexual freedom, the collective opprobrium she faced and the approval she merited, she was also writing, covertly, codedly, about her *pivotal*. Just as the whole of *The Second Sex* is about men as much as women, so too her essay on Brigitte Bardot is about Jean-Paul Sartre. Sartre was no Arthur Miller, Marilyn Monroe's consort and second husband, a smooth, graceful, catlike intellectual: his face wouldn't have looked out of place hanging on the outside of Notre Dame. But if his body was a mess, his mind was irresistible to a succession of young women of a philosophical bent. Beauvoir tolerated his polyvalent desires, claiming a disinterested curiosity in his attainments in bed. At the same time, she was bound to resent the women who seemed to get younger and prettier as she grew older and more lined. The final sentence of Beauvoir's essay expresses her anxiety about

BB's evolution: 'I hope that she will mature, but that she will not change.' But that unreasonable, impossible demand, which she would otherwise never articulate, corresponded absolutely to her image of Sartre.

We didn't need to read Simone de Beauvoir. BB was our Beauvoir. As in Paris, so too in Romford, there was fascination with the Bardot phenomenon, but again there were disagreements of interpretation. No one wanted to ban her films or excommunicate her, but there was, for example, heated debate at Jeff and Phil's over exactly how large her breasts were.

'Big enough to hang your hat on!' asserted John Griffin, Steve's big brother, who had introduced us to the two barbers.

'You could open up a dairy with them,' suggested Griffo.

'My bird's got bigger tits than that!' retorted Jeff as he razored John's neck. 'Fuckin' gigantic they are – like the Himalayas. Sometimes I get lost in there and can't find my way out. I'm going to take a sherpa with me next time.'

'36–20–34,' I quoted from memory. '8 stone 9 pounds. 5 feet 7 inches.' Her measurements were supposed to have remained cast in stone for years. But the statistics lied, since BB ballooned to the size of a billboard in our minds.

'QED,' said Jeff. '36 is nothing. 38 is minimum for me. D-cup. And 34 – peuh! – that's a boy's backside.'

The idea was scandalous. We – the Griffins and me – railed against the comparison of BB and a boy. We conceded that her buttocks were tight and muscular rather than massively rounded and agreed with Beauvoir that 'seen from behind, her slender, muscular dancer's body is almost androgynous', but still held firm to the corollary that 'femininity triumphs in her ravishing chest'. A solid form vs content argument. It was disturbing all the same to come into contact with an infidel. A creeping relativism was insidiously at work. Looking back on it, Jeff was probably the most sophisticated and prophetic commentator of the age. Years later on the West Coast, championed by Salvador Dalí, the legend took hold that Bardot had been born a man and was the beneficiary of an extremely successful sex-change operation. This would account alike for the boyish behind and the predatory sexual behaviour. Had not Vadim himself said that her 'tender derrière would have been the envy of Adonis and Aphrodite'?

Did not *Don Juan ou Et si Don Juan était une femme* suppose that Bardot had been male in a previous incarnation? Thank God Jeff and Phil didn't get wind of it.

> JEFF: What'd I tell you? I fuckin' told you her knockers weren't big enough!
> ANDY: [*inarticulate spluttering*]
> GRIFFO: Not as big as your mouth, for sure!
> JOHN: Bigger than your dick though!
> JEFF AND PHIL: [*cackling*] You've been had, boys.

But 1968, for Griffo and me, preceded sexual ambiguity. BB was woman, all woman and nothing but; the antithesis of man, she defined womanliness: how she was was how she should be.

'Why don't you bring your bird in then?' John Griffin proposed to Jeff, 'And I'll bring my tape measure along and we'll settle it.'

# 11

# The End of May 1968

Du Petit ABBCédaire
                        *Cahiers du cinéma*, May 1957

(A little alphaBBet)

John was a brutal empiricist, but Griffo and I were inclined to idealism. BB, we realized, was not reducible to a set of measurements, or to this or that photograph. She was not the first screen siren: setting aside my own flirtation with Monroe, Russell, Gardner, we were conscious of a long erotic tradition behind her, that would have included Rita Hayworth, Veronica Lake, Greta Garbo, possibly Mae West, and certainly *Playboy* Pets of the Year 1966 and 67, the familiars of Jeff and Phil's barber shop. But Bardot had given up the cosmetics and the stilettos and the phoney fidelity. BB became the Hegelian Idea. Every woman alluded to her, led us back to the source, the *fons et origo*. She was the unsurpassable Absolute who spared us the sweat and anguish of chasing after shadowy simulacra.

As BB was to physiology so St Tropez was to geography, which is why, when it came to doing a 'special project' in Mr Holmes's French classes, I picked the Riviera option. St Tropez stood out against a background of wealth and infamy, casinos and millionaire yachts, haute couture designers, industrialists, con-men and gigolos, or rather stood back from this foreground: the simple fishing village, the sea and La Madrague, a 'pocket-sized paradise' as Vadim described it. French was sandwiched between Religious Education and Ancient Greek and I obscurely jumbled up the Mediterranean and the Sea of Galilee, St Tropez and Troy, BB and Jesus Christ, Sachs, Sarne, Paris and Achilles, the disciples, Hector, Odysseus and me. In my mind, BB was a composite of Goldilocks, Helen, the Golden Fleece and Baude-laire's *Chevelure*, all musk and tar and slaves and sails. In fact, her classical credentials were impressive in both Latin and Greek: *Mio figlio Nerone* (*Nero's Mistress*; *Nero's Weekend*) (1956) casts her as Poppea, the Emperor's personal tutor in pleasure, wiser than Seneca; in *Helen of Troy* (1954), passed over for the title part, she is Andraste, Helen's handmaiden who stays behind in Greece; by the time of Godard's *Le Mépris* (1963), she has become a displaced synthesis of Helen and Penelope, with a dash of Cleopatra thrown in.

Bardot, bard-*eau*, poet of water. Bar-dough: a loaf of bread, a flask of wine and thou. She was a one-woman army of metaphors, metonyms and anthropomorphisms.

But she was a woman for all that. Just as well we didn't read Beauvoir too soon. Perhaps it is useless to make the acquain-tance of the young woman named Brigitte Bardot – and so it was if you were Simone de Beauvoir. Only Griffo's more practical, earthy genius was capable of grasping that St Tropez, unlike Troy, was actually on the map, that we could make our way there, and have knowledge of the Idea in person. But what will we do for money? We'll earn some. And what about transport? We'll hitch. And how do we find her? She'll find us. Without him, these self-evident truths might never have occurred to me. Griffo was the one who first understood that there was a world behind the words, a reality we could inhabit and have coitus with. And yet he was a poet at heart, with a semiotic sensitivity to language.

'*BB* – a mighty name, is it not?' Griffo panted one evening at his place between rounds of sparring, trying to stay sharp in case the Parrish brothers ambushed us. Pursuing some mystic pattern, we had come up with a list of stars with double initials, Marilyn Monroe, Greta Garbo, Claudia Cardinale, Doris Day, Simone Signoret, Lois Lane, but agreed that the letters BB somehow stood alone.

'Strictly, that should be pronounced *Bébé* – "baby".'

'What's the difference?'

'*Bébé* means something; *Bee Bee* doesn't.'

'Course it does. Let me dive into your hive, Bee Bee, I want your honey in my tummy. Do you want my honey in your

tummy? Buzz Buzz Buzz Buzz. Boobs Bum Bristols Backside . . .'
'Breasts Bosom Buttocks Body . . .'
'Big Bust Beer Bejabers . . .'
'Buxom Blonde Beastly Beatitudes . . .'
'Bollocks.'

A poster for *Le Mépris*, blue-tacked to my wall next to Napoleon's death mask, carries pictures of both BB and Jack Palance and is emblazoned with the message: 'BARDOT AT HER BOLD, BARE AND BRAZEN BEST (Revelling in Rome, cavorting in Capri . . . jolting even the jaded international jet-set in her pursuit of love!).' The alliteration was inescapable. Everything was visibly entwined, roped and troped: St Tropez and Romford, BB and us, chained together in an immense bracelet of b's, converging participants in some cosmic drama that was inexorably heading for a climax. In 'The God's Script', Jorge Luis Borges writes that 'there is no proposition that does not imply the entire universe; to say *the tiger* is to say the tigers that begot it, the deer and turtles devoured by it, the grass on which the deer fed, the earth that was mother to the grass, the heaven that gave birth to the earth. I considered that in the language of a god every word would enunciate that infinite concatenation of facts, and not in an implicit but in an explicit manner, and not progressively but instantaneously. In time, the notion of a divine sentence seemed puerile or blasphemous. A god, I reflected, ought to utter only a single word and in that word absolute fullness.' *BB* became our tiger, our alpha and omega, our aleph, our mantra, our microcosm. The letter B was an entire dictionary to us, an ABBC, a thesaurus of cabbalistic knowledge to be assimilated.

'To BB or not to BB, that is the question.'

'Look,' said Griffo, 'if you turn it this way round, you can draw nipples on it. Or . . . there – a pair of knickers.'

She made me think of Dieppe, that first time I set foot in a foreign land, a harbour with masts and funnels, flags and ropes and spinnakers, fish with silver scales, waiters with silver trays, cafés with tables and chairs outside, a gangway into a warmer, intenser sunlight, an express train thundering through the night to Spain. And, another time, of the train ride back to Victoria when a girl from Basingstoke asked me, 'Do you know what

French kissing is?' Until then I'd always thought it had something to do with General de Gaulle.

# 12

# June 1968

TRINTIGNANT: Il faudrait d'abord que je change de tête.
                                        *Et Dieu créa la femme*

(First of all I would need to change the way I look.)

Given that BB was the unadorned embodiment of the Real, it seems at first contradictory to be too anxious about Appearance. But we were. Sartre, coming to our rescue, explains that the real is nothing but the sum of appearances. Once we have overcome the illusion of the metaphysical reality-hidden-behind-appearance, then it is clear that 'the being of an existent is precisely what it *appears to be.*'

We counted on Brigitte to accept us for what we were and, at the same time, to transform us into what we ought to be. But we were still at the stage of becoming and we needed all the help we could get. The key to finding BB, to her finding us, was looking good. Yet the appearance of naturalness could only be achieved at the cost of immense pains.

The Bodger wasn't coming. Neither was the chocolate brown, no point *giving* him an edge. Our unspoken fear was that BB would choose between us, would select one but not the other, *him* and not *me*. We were a team, we stood together, but I knew he'd betray me if it came to the crunch. I'd betray him all right, in a flash: the end justified the means.

ANDY: Sorry, Griffo old man, but she says it's me she wants not you.
GRIFFO: Right you are, Andy. I'll be off then.
ANDY: *C'est la vie.*
GRIFFO: I'll shoot myself, of course. There's nothing left to live for now.

ANDY: Adieu, old friend!
GRIFFO: The best man won! [*Exits. A few seconds, then the retort of a single gunshot.*]

Griffo fought hard for the sheepskin – it had been such a winner – but was forced to admit that it would be *de trop* amid the tropic clime of St Tropez. In return I put aside the flower-power necklace (which had *loser* written all over it anyway). We wanted to travel light, so we cut our baggage down to essentials: cream flares, white painter's trousers, the single vent, Ravel brogues, sleeveless cardie, waiter's jacket, blue button-downs, Levi's Sta-Prest, khaki, Jaeger: our rucksacks were bulging with bare necessities. My precious copy of *Being and Nothingness* (in the Hazel E. Barnes translation, as new) was thrown in as a talisman.

Still we knew in our herringbones that our fate could hang by a tonik thread. So it was that the crimson shirt in Brent and Collins, the one with the cutback collar and double stitching around the cuffs, neck 15–and-a-half, 100% cotton, going for a fiver in the summer sale, assumed such significance in our planning. It was a beacon blazing out a message that the lighthouse-keeper's daughter (*Manina, la fille sans voiles*, 1952, or *The Girl in the Bikini* – 'the lighthouse keeper's daughter who believed in dressing light') could not fail to pick up on her radar. It was the key in the lock, the open sesame to BB's bed.

I saw it first. I know it was in the window and therefore, legally, anybody's, but morally, I had staked a claim. It was mine. I was already making my way back through the market to Stones to scrounge five pounds from my mother, who could be counted on to have flogged a couple more sewing machines and who would be relieved that for once the gear wasn't secondhand and I wasn't planning to dye anything. So when I ran into Griffo outside The Bull, it was only natural to crow about my find. Back in under five minutes, I swear, yet there in the window where once had been a shirt-sized sea of crimson was now an empty space, between the zip-up nylon windcheater (red and blue hoops on collar and cuffs) and the lavender three-piece (cotton tonik lookalike).

That shirt was my armour, my magic ring, my papers of

transit. It was gone, I was sunk. I dashed in, as if sheer brazen bullshitting could save me, as if a bold statement of intent would translate into truth. 'I've come for the shirt!' I announced, standing my ground before Johnny Evans, lanky ginger-haired Johnny, good old gorgeous groovy Johnny, a mate of Griffo's from Chase Cross, who had promised it to me five minutes before. 'The crimson one,' I added.

'Another geezer bagged it, sorry, guv.'

'But . . . I thought . . . you said . . .'

'Company policy, guv, can't reserve sale goods: *buy or bye-bye.*'

Bye-bye it would be then. Bye-Bye, BB. Those B's returned to haunt me, like the tolling of a bell. Griffo consoled me with half a drooping chocolate eclair in Stones.

'Don't be such a gloomy old sod, Andy,' he counselled cheerily. 'You won't even need the shirt – she'd just rip it off you. And then it's – Ballooning Bristols – Bulging Brassiere.'

The meaning of those fateful letters was undecidable, reversible, at once self-contained and open-ended. But I couldn't help feeling cheated just the same, as if I'd had my best chance snatched from under me.

A fortnight later I discovered who had got himself inside the shirt when Griffo wore it to our farewell party.

'Kept that pretty quiet, didn't you,' I said in my cheesecloth. 'Bastard. Bugger. Nick the shirt off my bloody back, wouldn't you. Would and did.'

'What? This is *that* shirt? Crimson? But this is more a burgundy or maroon or cerise. It's never crimson. How was I to know you were after it? What's the big deal anyway? Jaysus, man, it's only a shirt, isn't it?'

No. A shirt is never just a shirt. A shirt is destiny. I didn't know it then, but as it turned out, maybe I had misread the signs. That shirt was a jinx.

# 13

# June 1968 Continued

TRINTINGANT'S MOTHER: Au lieu de dire des bêtises, tu
  ferais mieux de travailler.
BARDOT: Mais je travaille. Je travaille à être heureuse.

*Et Dieu créa la femme*

(TRINTINGANT'S MOTHER: Instead of saying silly
  things, you would be better off finding some work to
  do.
BARDOT: But I am working. I'm working at being happy.)

We would have made exceptionally smooth millionaire playboys
strolling about in sockless Guccis with hair sprouting out of our
unbuttoned shirt fronts had it not been for the lack of millions.
But Sarne taught us that we could do without Bavarian castles,
Rollers, helicopters, Mediterranean powerboats, private Lear
jets, Christmas at St Moritz and New Year at Gstaad and
drinking Glühwein on the Wassengrat.

All we had to do was position ourselves under a palm tree on
the beach at St Tropez and wait for lightning to strike. We knew
that if we did but loiter long enough upon the shore then BB
would phut by on a small boat whose engine was just about to
break down and blow up and we, like Antoine in *And God
Created Woman*, would swim out and rescue her and swarm all
over her on the sand.

We just had to get down south. A hundred quid per man
ought to do it. At a quid a time, we would only have to wash a
hundred cars twice. Griffo's brother John gave us our first job
one Saturday, but we were in a hurry to get off to the Palais and
got the dosh up front and just chucked a bucket over his red
Renault with the reverse-hinged doors and gave it a quick
chamois and divvied up the cash. When we got back John was

gearing up for the evening shift. 'I thought you two were supposed to *clean* my motor,' he said. 'It's got more streaks on it than a fuckin' zebra.'

Griffo took to selling hot-dogs from Clive's mobile stall opposite St Edward the Confessor in the market place. He loved his work. He loved the aroma of fried onions and lashings of tomato sauce that wafted along the street like gas, the sizzle of bangers browning on the stove, the repartee with customers. 'Nice fat juicy long one,' he would rhapsodize, thrusting the dripping cylinder of fat between the jaws of the roll. Too bad the job only lasted till he was caught with his hand in the till. He was only borrowing the money from the float and was going to make it up that very same day. But by god that Clive was a hard man, and it was a crying shame what with as many sausages as you could eat too.

I wangled a spot myself outside The Pig and Pound where I had had my first drink with Griffo, loading and unloading a fruiterer's stall. 'A barrow, a bird and a tonik': that was Sid Heaviside's trinity, his triad. In Romford's class struggle, 'I've got a barrow' meant you'd arrived, on a level with 'I've got a hod'. I didn't have a barrow, though, and was looking at years before I worked my way up to yelling, 'Get your lovely nanas here, two bob a pound!' So it came as a relief to be given the push when I overslept one Saturday and didn't turn up until 5 am. In those days jobs were like conkers on the tree just waiting to be knocked down.

Once again Vadim – who started out as a photographer on *Paris-Match* before graduating to film director and Bardot consort – showed us the way. Along the London Road to the west of the crossroads, upstairs next to the Ind Coope brewery, was the headquarters of the *Romford Recorder*, 'The Voice of Romford'. We fancied ourselves as reporters swanning around on expense accounts, picking up scoops in bars and cafés, and having adventures like Tintin and more women than Bluebeard, so we walked through the front door one day and straight into a conference with the editor.

He was a kindly man in shirtsleeves and a loosened tie with golfballs on it who sat us in his office and organized us a cup of coffee too. 'Well, boys, now what are you good at?'

'Football,' said Griffo.

'You could write us a match report then,' said the editor. 'The season's a way off though. What are you doing for the summer?'

'We're going to St Tropez,' I said.

'Is that so?' said the editor, swivelling in his chair. 'Not going to meet Brigitte Bardot, are you, by any chance?'

'Why not?' I said.

'Now there's a scoop for you, an interview with the Sex Kitten herself. Think you could take some pics while you're at it?'

'Course,' said Griffo.

'That's settled then, you do me 500 words – no, make that 750 – on the Private Life of Brigitte Bardot, plus pictures, and I'll pay you – how does £25 sound?'

'Great,' I said.

'Each?' said Griffo.

'*Each*,' said the editor.

We had got ourselves a real job now. I would do the writing and Griffo, we agreed, would take the pictures with John's Kodak. Psychologically, we were ahead, but there was no money up front and we had still barely opened our accounts.

'You ever think about modelling?' Griffo said, one fine day, when we were leafing through a glossy magazine in his kitchen eating his Mum's soda bread. 'Will you look at these geezers? Like falling off a log and think of the clobber.' Griffo told me about a mate of his who was the son of a tailor and had thirty-six suits in his wardrobe – Prince of Wales, tweed, linen, mohair, worsted, patch pockets, flaps, double-breasted with broad lapels, no lapels, three-piece, two-piece, three-button, two-button, four-button, one-button, turn-ups, flares, straights, tapers, herring-bone, keypocket, all the colours of the rainbow, and several shades of grey (but suave), Norfolk jacket, gaping double vents like the Baron, no vents like the Saint, pinstripe, plain, triple pleats – and he'd been walking down Oxford Street and he'd been spotted and offered a job straight off just on the strength of his suit, although which one was unknown.

That was the lure of modelling: all those hopes and plans and schemes and dreams, they were all already somehow expressed in the singular cut of the cloth, the fall of the trouser leg over a gleaming shoe, a shot cuff and a pocket handkerchief, the fringe of hair draped over the sharp line of the collar, the knotted trenchcoat belt and the raised lapels.

'Thirty-six is what it used to be,' said Griffo, 'It's gone up to forty or fifty now, for sure.'

The name was in the magazine and we got the number off the operator. 'Hello Estelle Davis Modelling Agency how may I help you?' It was a refined sort of voice at the other end, the sort that would have long varnished fingernails attached to it. I asked her about vacancies for two and assured her that we had done a bit of modelling before, in Paris, for *Jardin des modes*.

'How old are you exactly, you and your friend?'

'Sixteen . . .'

'Eighteen,' chipped in Griffo, his ear next to mine.

'Is that sixteen or eighteen?'

'Eighteen, yes, eighteen. Six foot, blond, blue eyes. Griffo's got red hair. Looks like Paul McCartney. I'm more . . .'

'John Lennon? Send us your portfolios and we'll put you on file.'

'Fine, thank you,' I said.

'Hey! What about the gear?' Griffo cut in, yanking the receiver from my hand. 'The clothes, sweetheart, d'we get to keep them or not? . . . Right, well, fuck you then!' He slammed the phone down in the cradle. 'Wankers! "We're not in the business of giving things away,"' he whined in a bitter falsetto.

To hell with portfolios, we weren't going to sit around in any drawer hoping to be plucked out of oblivion, we couldn't wait that long. So instead we humped crates for Stenhouse Catering on Saturday afternoons. Weddings were our speciality. We would unload a hundred place settings from the back of a lorry and lug them into a church hall, and then come back in the evening and collect the empties, spending most of our wages at Stones in-between. We made a point of looking thirsty the second time round, which wasn't difficult after ten or fifteen matrimonials manhandling tons of crockery up and down staircases. 'Here, mate, want a drink?' some good samaritan would say.

Every so often we would intersect with departing newlyweds. 'Lucky bastard!' Griffo would say admiringly. 'Body and a half on that one.' Or, 'Poor old sod! Built like a cement mixer, she is.' He awarded a 'goer of the day' prize or prizes. Not all wedding parties were happy wedding parties, though. You could smell it and hear it as you came through the door and you wouldn't want to stay but you'd be pulled in anyway. 'Have a fuckin' drink, will ya.' The bride would be pregnant and the groom pissed.

'I'm never getting married,' Griffo said. 'God help me if I do.' Other times he'd wax poetic. 'A fortnight dipping your wick into that! It'd drop right off, so it would.'

As we cycled home late at night, bowling along tidy Avenues, Crescents, Gardens, under the street lamps of housing estates, we imagined ourselves flying over the darkened houses and peeling back the rooftops. 'Think of it! The rutting that must be going on right now, right under our noses.' The mystery of sexual congress conferred a magical radiance on the most ordinary of people, neighbours, newsagents, the postman, but especially the post-woman, who all inhabited a parallel universe right alongside our own, occupying the very same space and in all other respects identical, but from which we were rigorously excluded.

But it was as builder's mates that we began to accumulate our stake. 'I need some big strapping boys like the two of ye's,' Griffo's father said to us. We were also cheap.

Gerry Griffin had a soft spot for me because of my fair hair and blue eyes. 'Do you have any German blood in ye?' he would ask from time to time. 'A fine race of men they be.' And at other times he would say, 'I hate the feckin' Germans. Why wouldn't I when they bombed the shite out of Romford?' But if his opinions were constantly changing, they all carried equal conviction and were delivered with the same indiscriminate intensity.

We were drafted in to lay a warehouse floor next to the football stadium, walking the plank in and out of a skip, barrowing hardcore, hammering it into dust, shovelling wet cement on top and tamping it smooth. Griffo spent too much time resting his elbows on his spade, according to his father, and I sank for all time in Mr Griffin's estimation when he asked me to fetch him a monkey wrench from his tool box and I came away from it empty-handed. 'All that fine schooling ye have, and what good did it do ye?' he railed, and it didn't help that he eventually found the wrench behind a stack of bricks where he had left it. 'Can I not depend on ye's ever to put things back where they came from?'

So it was that we were farmed out to John to put in the footings for some houses in Shenfield. John Griffin was only four or five years older than us, but those years represented a well-stocked whorehouse of experience. He was the smoothest, most sophisticated male we knew, the real Gunther Sachs of Romford, a charismatic playboy with bottomless funds, a style king who had his clothes tailormade and had already written off two or three cars, including a green Cinquecento and a red Mercedes SL 190 convertible. He totalled them on Fridays to let off a bit of steam.

John had once gone to a party at a judge's house in Gidea Park and swung on a chandelier. 'D'you ever see Johnny Weismuller do this?' he said, and pulled the ceiling to the ground. He offered to rebuild it, but was turned down flat. Not only that, but he had perfected a bloodcurdling scream that was a cross between a police siren and a Frank Ifield yodel. Every now and then he would wind down the window of his car and let one rip and terrify the living daylights out of people. When he went back to the west coast of Ireland he would always take a couple of gross of Durex with him and come back boasting of the bundle he'd made.

'Jay*ay*sus!' he burst out the time the three of us were barrelling back home along the A12 and we had been drinking and singing and in a moment of uncustomary honesty we let slip the truth of our condition. 'D'ye mean you lads haven't had your way with a woman yet? Why didn't you say so before? Uncle Johnny'll fix you up – satisfaction guaranteed or your money back!'

Ultimately, my parents chipped in £50. They were frankly relieved I was clearing off to France: it would be good for my O-level French. And at least it would get me away from that dreadful boy Griffin.

# 14

## One Saturday Night at the End of June 1968

And I tried . . . And I tried . . . And I tried . . . And I
tried

Rolling Stones, 'Satisfaction'

John had cornered the job just by walking into Foster's site office. He had an innocent face, clean-shaven and unmarked, except for a few strategic freckles, and a square jaw. It was the perfect disguise.

'How many vehicles do you have?'

'I have a fleet of lorries.'

'How much machinery?'

'I have five JCBs, a bulldozer and a cat.'

'Men?'

'I can have a hundred here in the morning, but I won't be needing that many.'

He couldn't afford to hire a JCB to do the heavy work of digging and clearing, so we had to do it, Griffo and I, a lot more slowly. It wasn't so much that John was lying, he was just a great believer in the power of the shovel. When a lorryload of bricks was delivered, the driver wanted five quid on the side to lift them off with the crane, which by rights he should have been doing anyway. John got us to take them all off by hand while the driver stood there unmoved.

'I'm not putting money in the pocket of a thief,' he thundered, and claimed a moral victory.

What with labouring like Sisyphus and us without even a hod, it was inevitable we should skimp on some of the finer details, like digging foundations. 'There'll be a lawn sprouting up through the Axminster in a few months,' I said, feeling a twinge of guilt while we cemented the grass into place as if we were slapping on Brylcreem.

John laughed. 'Andy, you're a smart lad. Now what do you think we have mowers for?'

It was in the course of excavating trenches and mixing cement that we unfolded our plans before him. We wanted his admiration and got it. 'She's a fine woman. You cannot do better than Brigitte herself.' He made it sound as if they were old friends. 'I'd like to be there just for the crack. By God, lads, you cannot go down to Saint-Trope with no practice beforehand, you'll not be fit.'

It made sense. Vadim himself had had his actress in the hayloft well before he ever met BB. We didn't want to make fools of ourselves when the trousers were down. We were organizing a farewell rave-up at Griffo's place which John re-christened our 'Goodbye Virginity' party. He promised us he'd have a bird waiting in his bedroom and she was all ours. She wouldn't mind helping out two lads in distress, no, it'd be a pleasure. And no, she had no prejudices about age, young or old, she wasn't fussy. She just couldn't get enough of it.

'What's she like then, this bird?' Griffo said, as we stopped for a thermos. He'd been giving the matter some serious thought while digging. 'Not one of your rats, is she?'

'Boys,' John said in his infinite wisdom, 'you cannot have Brigitte Bardot before you have Brigitte Bardot. And this Jane is no Brigitte Bardot, but she's no monster either, I'm telling you. The fact is, she's a bit of a scrubber, but none the worse for that.' John promised us it was all fixed.

But he had anxieties of his own. 'Now are you sure you boys know what you're doing of?' he queried on the way back down the A12. 'We wouldn't want Jane pissing herself on account of yous. Would you be needing any practical tips on the how-to?'

But even Griffo had taken careful notes in biology class. And we had Dave Berry, an inspired inside-right planning on a career in the hotel trade, to fill in the gaps. We listened open-mouthed as he replayed his technique with a girl named Chrissie who would do anything. 'You shove it all the way in, see, like cleaning a chimney,' he said. 'I have to stop when she starts choking though.' Dave used to worry when he couldn't get a hard-on: 'Must have been overdoing it. Better give it a rest tonight.' He blamed the decline of his footballing abilities on too much sex. But it seemed to us a price worth paying.

We weren't overkeen on the 'Goodbye Virginity' tag, so we called it 'Wembley Night' or 'the Cup Final'. As the moment of truth approached we were as psyched up as new caps pacing the dressing-room before they jog out on the pitch.

'You fit then?' Griffo said.

'Never fitter,' I said.

'I can see you scoring tonight.'

'I reckon you might pop one between the posts yourself.'

The score was four–two on Saturday morning in the five-a-side game at Rise Park, with Martin and Griffin among the goals. We took that as a good omen. It was going to be a massacre, a walkover, ten–nil on the night.

At the Griffin house, a semi opposite the shops in Gobions Avenue, the parents were out and the supplies were in. A crate of Ind Coope for a float, peanuts, crisps – salt and vinegar, cheese and onion – and a plastic sign we had hung on the wall reading 'Way Out', with a pointing hand beneath it. Griffo stood by the door with a wooden ruler and measured the height of skirts above the knee. If they didn't meet the minimum requirement of eight inches they were turned away. You had to have standards, you couldn't let just anybody in. Evening dress for men was flares. Headbands and cow bells were optional extras.

'Are you set, you boys?' John said. He had holed up in a corner with Jane on his lap. We couldn't see much of her face, since it was tucked behind John's ear, but she had long long legs and wore tight bleached Levis, the kind you shrank onto your legs in the bath, and a white crimplene top through which, at the right angle, you could cop an eyeful of an amply filled bra.

'What do you think of her, looks-wise?' I asked.

'Fuck the looks!' Griffo replied.

Nick and Ron, from Hornchurch, had brought their 45s collection and we piled on the records ten at a time. It was a High Fidelity record player, the kind where if you left the arm up the pick-up would automatically return to the beginning over and over again. *'I can't GET no (wah-wah-wah) satisFACtion,'* Mick Jagger groaned repeatedly, speaking on behalf and precisely echoing the thoughts, the thought, the only thought, of ninety-nine per cent of the teenage males chanting and writhing in the front room.

There was still a half-hour of virginity to endure, and we ticked off the seconds chatting up a couple of girls from round King's Hill called Sylvie and Carol, who were friends of Kathy's. But our hearts weren't really in it. We had our minds on higher things: upstairs at midnight.

'*You're all I need to get by*,' crooned Marvin Gaye and Tammi Terrell. '*You are everything and everything is you*.'

Vicky Songhurst had brought along a cake with the words 'AU REVOIR, STEVE' iced on top. So we had some of that. I was pissed she hadn't put 'ANDY' on it too. Downstairs was agony, but we enjoyed our suffering – as if it would refine and toughen and justify us – conscious as we were of the imminence of paradise. I remember the Drifters singing 'Up On the Roof' as the hands on the electric clock over the fireplace finally joined up and at last became fully vertical. We scrambled up the stairs, each trying to hold the other back.

For all the time we had spent anticipating this moment, we had never once thought about it in hard, practical terms. One question that had not occurred to us was: who should go first? It occurred to us now. We debated the issue in a nervy whisper outside the bedroom door. First we both wanted to go first. Griffo had powerful arguments on his side: it was his house, it was his bedroom, John was his brother. Moreover, he was a month older, so his need was greater: surely I could wait another month?

'OK,' I gave in, 'you go first.'

'Right,' he said.

'Go on then.'

'I was thinking. By rights it ought to be you.'

'What?'

'Be my guest. It's only polite. After you.'

'No, after you.'

'Look, let's toss for it, that's fair.'

'All right,' I agreed, 'let's toss.'

But we hadn't a coin between us.

'I've got an idea,' I said.

'What's that?'

'Let's go in together.'

'Andy, didn't I always say you were a flippin' genius?'

We took a deep breath. This was it then. The turning point, the hayloft of truth, the threshold of manhood. Beyond the door lay the unhooked, the unzipped, the unlaced, the unbuttoned and the unhinged, which would undo us for all time.

There is a legend that Pilou had taken Vadim to his desk, unlocked the drawer and shown him a pistol. 'If you lay a finger on my daughter I shall not hesitate to use this on you.' Had he but known, he would have shot the jolly Roger through the heart there and then, for it was already too late. It had fallen to this unreliable drifter, a graduate – along with Marcel Marceau – of the Charles Dullin drama school, the youngest screenwriter in Europe and perhaps the world, the man who had coined the term 'discothèque', to defile Brigitte. It must have been love: he had foregone the opportunity to join a lonely Leslie Caron in Hollywood (shooting *An American in Paris*) on her account. According to Vadim, it was at Christian Marquand's studio on the second floor of 15 rue de Bassano, just off the Champs Elysées, in the sultry summer of 1950 (which would make her only fifteen), that BB threw open the traditional green shutters and cried out to astonished passers-by, 'At last – I am a woman!'

We said nothing as we knocked quietly on the door and swung it open. From out of the shadows, two huge buttocks shone in the light of the moon. They were John's. 'What kept you boys?' he scolded us, grinding away gently into the darkness beneath him.

'You said midnight,' said Griffo.

'It's gone midnight.'

'Only just.'

'She couldn't wait any longer.'

'It's only a minute past twelve.'

'You'd better come back in a half hour.'

'Twelve-thirty, then.'

'Be gone now, man.'

We withdrew.

'Forty-four seconds,' said Ron. He was sitting at the top of the stairs consulting his watch. 'That must be some sort of record. Didn't you bother taking your togs off?'

'There's been a bit of a hold-up,' I said.

'Ron, why don't you fuck off back to Hornchurch,' said Griffo.

By half-twelve, John had still not appeared. 'The booger,' Griffo said. We gave him another five minutes, then Griffo went in and closed the door behind him. The door opened again and Griffo came out. 'Says she won't let him go, she's got him by the balls, he's trapped, but there'll be other nights. The bastard. Says what are we worrying about, when we've got Brigitte Bardot all lined up?'

## PART TWO

# Love

'C'est là ce que nous avons eu de meilleur!' dit Frédéric.
'Oui, peut-être bien? C'est là ce que nous avons eu de
   meilleur!' dit Deslauriers.

Flaubert, *L'Education sentimentale*

('That was the best time of our lives!' said Frédéric.
'Do you think so? Yes, that was the best time of
   our lives!' said Deslauriers.

Flaubert, *A Sentimental Education*)

# The Beginning of the Second Week of July 1968

We've seen it in the movies,
now let's see if it's true.

Cliff Richard, *Summer Holiday*

John ferried us down to Dover in his wide-wheeled Beetle, largely out of a sense of guilt. 'Boys, now be fair, what could I do? There was no stopping her. She was going like a train.'

As we approached the terminal, John fished in his glove compartment. 'Next best thing,' he said, stuffing a six-pack of Durex gossamer into our outstretched hands. 'Do you think that'll be enough for the pair of you?'

'It'll get us started,' Griffo said.

'Bring us back her bikini, just to prove you made it.'

'Who says we're coming back?' I said. 'There'll be no stopping her.'

We couldn't see beyond Bardot, who blocked the view like a mountain. As in Jules Verne's *Rocket to the Moon*, the departing Bardonauts had never contemplated the return half of the journey. 'The question [of how to get back to earth] is of no immediate interest,' Barbicane proudly declared, dismissing this craven thought. 'Later when we judge it to be the right moment to return we shall consider the matter.'

Our bitterness with John didn't last. Maybe, we rationalized, as we boarded the boat, it had all been for the best: this way we were still fresh, still hungry, still fifteen-year-old virgins. John Lennon had proclaimed his love for Yoko Ono and we were now more confident than ever.

All journeys are half-flight, half-quest. In *Doctor at Sea* (a pre-Vadim film, which we saw after *And God Created Woman*) Dr Dirk Bogarde, on the run from a senior consultant's daughter, signs on the cargo-steamer *Lotus*, bound for Bellos (which looks like the Hollywood idea of Casablanca or Algiers) and finds Brigitte Bardot in his shower. It was too much to hope for on the Dover–Boulogne ferry, we didn't even have a shower, but we scoured the boat all the same, just in case.

Although Bogarde is technically the doctor, it is BB (with short red curls) who plays the role of therapist. Men with crooked backs straighten up at her approach, an appendectomy case makes an amazing recovery, and Dirk Bogarde, whose sexuality is placed in doubt alongside more explicit heterosexuals among the sailors and – it is hinted – may find a homosexual draw in the navy, is restored to fully functioning manhood. Her first words to him are 'I love you, love you, love you' – she is a night-club *chanteuse*, coupled as usual with a black orchestra – but it takes the whole voyage before they embrace unreservedly and agree to sail away to Rio together in the last scene (which accounts for the French title, *Rendezvous à Rio*).

But BB too is transformed by the film: by requiring her to speak throughout (with the exception of such phrases as *bon voyage*) in English, it reveals for the first time that *she has a French accent*. Hidden among other French accents, and disguised by speaking French, this secret truth had been hitherto concealed from us. She became at once more different, strange and therefore desirable, but also more accessible, since at the same time it was clear she spoke perfectly adequate English.

Like Dirk Bogarde, Griffo and I were running away: from Romford, England, our childhood, ourselves, and especially John and Jane, into the arms of the foreign, the unknown, BB. Britain forced us to be islands, isolated, cut off from our fellow human beings – especially girls – and alienated from our own instincts. The Continent could be counted on to connect us up. It was hard, looking behind us, over the stiff, starchy white cliffs of the reality principle and back up the A2, to believe that anyone ever had sex in England. The 'swinging sixties' was just a myth, a conspiracy to deceive, we had been the victims of what Marcuse denounced as 'surplus repression'. Ahead of us, across the Channel, over the horizon, in the land of pleasure, everything we had been missing out on lay in readiness, spread out before us like a Sunday picnic. Britain was a kind of Alcatraz, an off-shore penal colony of Europe. France, on the other hand, was not just another country, it was another planet.

Any idea of conquest, a settling of accounts for 1066, was far from our minds. It was we who wanted to be conquered all over again, our resistance overcome, carried off, ravished. We were steaming away from England, but it seemed to us on that still, sultry, glittering day in late July that it was France that was already making advances towards us, thrusting herself upon our attention, telling us 'I love you, love you, love you.'

There was no wind, there were no waves. Seated on one of the bow benches, rucksacks pillowing our feet, with no sense of motion, at most a gentle rocking, as if cradled in a hammock, we dreamily perceived the Normandy coast swimming out to greet us, like hospitable Hawaiian *wahine* surfing Captain Cook and his crew ashore.

From north-west down to south-east, we could feel sheer gravity dragging our mass down across the buxom blessed body of France, from head to tail, accelerating us towards the Mediterranean and the centre of the earth.

# 16

## The Same Evening

The only hope is dope.
Timothy Leary, *The Politics of Ecstasy*

As our feet touched down abroad, on the dock at Boulogne, the sky was the colour of Griffo's crimson shirt. 'St Tropez or die!' Griffo bellowed. We would have cut open our flesh and mingled our blood to cement our faith and eternal friendship, but we had omitted to bring razor blades, so contented ourselves with shaking hands and marched on in the dimming light, across the railway tracks and over the bridge, following the signs marked 'Auberge de la Jeunesse'.

'Well we made it!' Griffo said, as we tramped along past *boulangerie, patisserie, confiserie*, past delicate architectures of pastry cascading with chocolate and cream, past baguette and croissant, *pain au chocolat* and *mille feuilles*, past Camembert, Brie, Roquefort, *chèvre*, past dripping heads and torsos of butchered animals. 'Let's celebrate, eh?'

'Hadn't we better get to the youth hostel first?'

'Here, look, "Café-Bar".' A wide band of light striped the pavement outside, like a beach; the air was perfumed with a bouquet of ground coffee beans and Gauloises superimposed on the underlying tang of the sea. I sniffed it all in like one of that mythic olfactory race cited by Claude Lévi-Strauss who nourish themselves on smells alone.

'Come on, just to wet the whistle,' Griffo said. 'I'm getting tired of lugging this great sack around.'

'Christ, we only just got off the boat.'

'Stop being such a Protestant, Andy. You're in a good Catholic country now.'

We sat down at an outdoor table and took a look at the

Cannes, 1953

BB is born. So am I.

**Camber Sands, 1961**

The *coup de foudre.*

London, 1963

BB on the set of *Adorable Idiot*.
I am playing football with Griffo.

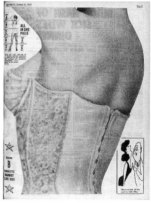

' A woman is not born but made.' (Simone de Beauvoir)

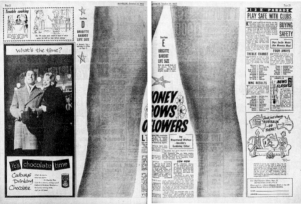

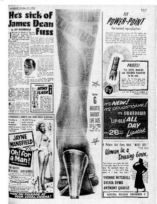

**London, 1966, prior to *Two Weeks in September***

A cigarette in one hand, a man in the other.
Which will last longer?

Mike Sarne                Gunter Sachs

Griffo                          Goat

**Some of my rivals**

Romeo, 1960s, spending the night.

Castrato, late '80s, sexually depleted.

**The dream and the nightmare**

menu. The cheapest thing on it was 'vin de table' so we ordered some of that. Fishing smacks and ferries sailed in and out of the harbour mouth, Renaults and Citroëns and Peugeots arced around the dock perimeter, and other customers came and went. At the table next to ours, two French women in pale jackets (vanilla? lemon?) and tapering dark skirts (navy or black) sat down and crossed their legs and ordered *cafés au lait*. In their twenties, fashion models perhaps, or advertising executives, or the mistresses of Marseillais gangsters. One of them smoked a long thin cigarette.

'Will you look at that!' said Griffo between gulps of purple wine. 'We've only been here five minutes and we're already surrounded.' He looked pensive. 'It's true, then, there are more beautiful women in France. Show me two birds like that walking down Romford High Street! Check those stockings – sheer. No holes. And the shirt. Not a see-through, but not a woolly either.' He sighed. 'It was worth it just for this. Reckon you can give them the old chat – in French, I mean?' He buttoned the top button of his army-surplus jacket.

'Come on, let's get to the hostel before it fills up or closes for the night.' It was too soon. I wasn't ready.

'*Bonjour!*' Griffo boomed at the two women and slid his chair over to their table. The 'j' was way too hard and the final 'r' completely unsounded, but the word was, overall, quite intelligible.

'*Bonsoir*,' replied the woman with the cigarette.

Griffo, stymied, turned to me for back-up. I pulled up my chair. '*Vous venez ici souvent?*' I said. It was awkward, I knew, but it was the best I could come up with on the spot: a literal rendering of our habitual line at the Palais. Too feeble by half for Griffo, who didn't even wait for their reply.

'*Vous*,' he gestured theatrically, kissing his fingertips, '*belles*.' Howler! Premature eulogy. Classic example of what not to do.

'*Merci*,' said the cigarette, smiling.

'*Michèle, ma belle*,' he crooned, '*sont les mots qui vont très bien ensemble, très bien ensemble . . .*'

Griffo's resemblance to Paul McCartney stopped short of his voice. Moreover it occurred to me that, strictly speaking, the Beatles should have written '*Ce* sont *des* mots . . .'

'I love you, I love you, I love you,' he wailed, encouraged. '*Parlez-vous anglais?*'

'*Naturellement*,' said the other one. 'We *are* English.'

'You mean you're not French? Holy Jesus, I thought you were French!'

Their names were Shelley and Jacqui and they were about to get on the same boat we had just got off. Returning home to Croydon after a one-day shopping trip to Boulogne. They worked in insurance at Liverpool Street and were quite chuffed to be taken for French women. To be fair, it was the kind of mistake anyone might make.

'They weren't even that much to look at,' Griffo said, as we trudged up the hill towards the *auberge de la jeunesse*.

'Not when you got close-up.'

'And the light wasn't too good.'

We were still too close to England, that was the trouble. Boulogne was, after all, Bouloyne, a neighbour of Dover and Folkestone, with just a narrow strip of water dividing them. Once all this was England anyway, or Kent was all France. Either way, there was room for confusion. France, the real France, started somewhere further south. There, surely, everything would be made clear. There, surely, we would be men at last.

We picked up a bottle of wine at an *épicerie*. It would have been silly not to, it was so cheap. With the aid of a penknife with a corkscrew attachment my father had loaned me, I winkled out the cork and we took it in turns to take a swig. It had a burnt, bitter, suffocating taste, like drinking smoke. 'Good stuff, eh?' said Griffo.

We pitched up at the youth hostel. There were still beds going. We dumped our packs upstairs next to our bunk. In the dining-room we ate some slightly squashed hard-boiled eggs we had brought with us. A couple of smartly dressed blokes came up to us and asked us in accented English where we were from. Their names were Yusuf and Mamet. They were from Marrakesh. Yusuf was tall, with a neat chin beard and moustache, and wore a creamy cotton jacket with patch pockets over Levis. Mamet was shorter, with whispy sideburns, and an orange bandanna and a silk waistcoat. Both had long, dark hair which fell tidily on their shoulders. They made Griffo and me, in our khaki, feel suddenly shabby and outmoded.

'Why do you come to France?' Yusuf said.

'We're going to see Brigitte Bardot,' Griffo said.

'A very beautiful woman,' Yusuf said.

'We were in St Tropez last month,' Mamet said. 'St Tropez, Nice, Cannes. The Riviera.'

'We saw *Bébé* on the beach,' said Yusuf. 'She is always on the beach.'

'She's easy to meet then?' Griffo said.

'No problem,' Yusuf said. 'Come. We must celebrate your arrival in France.'

'I've had enough to drink, thanks,' I said.

'No drink,' Mamet said. 'Look.' He dug down into his pocket and came up with a small twist of silver foil, which he untwisted and opened out in his hand. In it lay a cube of dry, earthy material.

'All the way from Marrakesh,' said Yusuf. 'Hashish – *merde* – very pure.' He frowned at a group of hearty Scandinavians who were too close to our table for comfort. He lowered his voice. 'This is very popular in England, no?'

'Sure thing,' Griffo agreed.

'How much in London?'

We looked blank. The strongest drug either of us had experimented with was a tinful of Old Ship tobacco in cigarettes rolled with liquorice paper among the trees of Raphael's Park.

'Five pounds an ounce?' suggested Mamet.

'Oh, at least,' I said.

'More like ten in London,' Griffo said.

Yusuf smiled warmly at us, as if we were personally responsible for the price rise. 'Here, come,' he said.

We followed. This was what we had come for: we weren't even out of Boulogne yet and already we were being offered a whiff of nirvana. Yusuf led us downstairs and out into the garden.

Mamet constructed the joint under the watchful eye of Yusuf: the tube, the tobacco, the sprinkling of powdered hashish, the twist in the embouchure – each movement precise and economical, like a watchmaker. Yusuf took out a lighter from his inside pocket.

We sat cross-legged and passed the joint around. When we sucked, the smouldering tip glowed in the darkness. Yusuf and Mamet seemed to emit no exhaust at all. Griffo and I inhaled deeply, modelling our technique on theirs.

'Sex with hashish,' said Yusuf, 'is like a perfect dream.'

'It is so beautiful,' added Mamet.

'I bet,' said Griffo. 'Ah, now if you were only girls!' He roared and slapped Yusuf on the back.

'Yes,' Yusuf coughed. 'If only.'

'Here you are, love, here's my hookah, suck on this.' Griffo rolled on the ground in mirth.

'Have a puff!' I chipped in wittily and fell on top of him and we rolled together on the grass and the tears came to our eyes. God, we were funny.

'And do you never make love with other boys in England?'

'What do you take us for? Queers?' Griffo sprawled again in helpless laughter.

'Pervs?' I echoed and lay back on the grass, exhausted with hilarity.

'Bum-bashers?' Griffo howled up at the moon.

When we pulled ourselves round, Yusuf and Mamet had vanished noiselessly into the night. We wandered off and soon found ourselves back at the docks.

'They say this stuff gives you visions,' I said. 'Supposed to open the doors of perception.'

'You reckon you can see God with it?' Griffo said.

We scanned the harbour. We could see a ferry. Two funnels. A crane. Silhouettes. We sat down soberly on the dockside to introspect.

'How're you feeling?' Griffo said.

'Headache,' I said. 'You?'

'Guts-ache.'

It was too much effort to sit up, so we lay down, and stuck our heads out over the harbour wall, hoping for some insight into our altered state from the water ten feet below. But the surface gleamed iridescently back at us, impenetrable, slick with oil, pitted with obscure lumps of detritus.

'I'm feeling seasick,' Griffo moaned. 'Woooo.' His mouth gaped and a torrent gushed forth into the shadows. It was like watching someone else yawning, I couldn't help myself. Then there were two, both of us lying there on the quayside, our heads jutting out over the water, like a couple of bath taps, pouring out our insides, finding relief in an emission quite different from what we'd had in mind.

# 17

# July 8

### Through the Star Gate
Arthur C. Clarke/Stanley Kubrick, *2001, A Space Odyssey*

In a story that appeared in the magazine *Strange Worlds*, c. 1959, and that I read in the early sixties, an earthling lands on a faraway planet that is a fabulous treasure-trove of (a) treasure; (b) secrets about the universe; not to mention (c) comely female aliens – all of it freely and readily available to any visiting spaceman. On one condition. First you have to pass a simple test, an initiation to demonstrate that you are worthy to enter and learn. Many had come to sit the test; none had passed. The failures were atomized or dropped into a bottomless pit; worse still would be to wander the cosmos forever tormented by the knowledge of having failed.

The test is deceptively straightforward. All around are futuristic anti-gravity towers hovering in mid-air, and flying saucers whirring by, the accoutrements of a technologically and morally superior civilization; but the test itself consists of a plain wooden building, a mere barn, a shack, with two doors: one, at one end, the entrance, the other, at the opposite end, the exit. The challenge – at once child's play and complex beyond imagining – is to walk in one door and walk out the other.

Challengers from the four corners of the galaxy are queueing up to take the test. Each in turn walks through the door and closes it behind him. Each in turn emerges from the same door, unable to make it to the exit just ten yards away. The most dazzling intellects over a radius of one hundred light years, some with brains the size of pumpkins, some nothing but pure brain being wheeled around in a vat, crackling with supercharged synapses, are forced to admit defeat: all enter and leave from one and the same door.

One scientist boldly postulates a space–time lesion that would have the effect of making the barn, of modest dimensions on the outside, infinite on the inside. Another ascribes the effects to a molecular magnetic drive or particle deflector or quantum warp. The aliens, who have a good sense of humour, laugh their ample, antennaed heads off at each of these way-off and way-out hypotheses.

At last it is the earthman's turn. After the universe's finest have tried and failed, no one would bet a single measly interstellar dollar on his chances. Earthlings have a reputation throughout the Milky Way as heroic no-hopers, and intellectually under-developed to boot. The aliens are polite, but already inwardly chuckling; others are cruelly mocking. The earthman walks up to the door, opens it and steps inside the conundrum.

Five seconds later he walks out again – *through the other door*! A dozen disparate creatures gape and gaze upon him with astonishment and respect, babbling into their universal transla-tors. The earthling throws open the door and shines a torch inside and reveals the elementary mechanism that everyone else had been too sophisticated and subtle to guess at: the floor of the building is nothing other than a treadmill. For every pace the challengers walked forwards the floor compensated by rolling them exactly one pace backwards, so that they remained always on the same spot. Only a transcendent and cunning alien intelligence or a primitive and practical earthling mind could have dreamed of such a crude but effective trick. It is not explained how the earthman manages to escape the treadmill: perhaps by clinging to the ceiling or the walls or by polevaulting himself over the obstacle. But the story ends with our hero being carried off by the enraptured aliens, who have at last found a fit recipient of their largesse. Indescribable pleasure, knowledge and power await him.

Boulogne was our barn. We waited an hour for a lift, two hours, three. Nothing. Nothing but snooty aliens looking down their noses and sniggering at us. We were fool enough not only to have both of us hitching, but to leave our two rucksacks plainly visible as well. We might as well have been trying to get a lift for four. In the first phase, we forgave those that left us standing on the kerb. In the second, our beckoning thumbs turned to clenched fists as cars sped unheedingly by. In the third, we openly threatened any vehicles that came near.

But, backward earthlings that we were, we managed to overcome paralysis in the end by the ingenious method of putting one foot in front of the other, and now we were running free. Even our packs seemed lighter. In fact, they were lighter: the shirts we had carefully washed (after their night on the dock) and hung on the line outside to dry, had vanished.

'God I loved that shirt,' grieved Griffo, after he had verbally cut the crimson throat of the thief who stole it.

'I loved it too,' I chimed in.

'Maybe we're better off without it.'

Tears sprang to my eyes. That shirt was a Jonah, a bloody anchor round our legs, an evil genie. Now at last we were delivered of the curse. Whoever is wearing it may be vomiting in Boulogne still.

We took the PARIS sign for a good omen and stuck out our thumbs. We would scarcely have been surprised had the driver turned out to be Brigitte Bardot herself, just asking for amorous stowaways in her crazy 2CV (*La Bride sur le cou*, 1961). As it was, he was the next best thing: the owner of a Citroën DS 19. The car stopped, curtseyed, flapped open the door with a sigh and we dived in, Griffo and the rucksacks on the back seat, me in front.

Jet black, spotless, sleek and slicked back, polished like a mirror. Just as BB was *Bébé* in France, so, similarly, DS was not just the meaningless 'DS' but rather *déesse* (or 'goddess'). The DS was less a motor vehicle than a flying saucer in conception. It reminded me of the monolith in *2001, A Space Odyssey*: an exercise in seamlessness, the souvenir of an incalculably advanced civilization, an impeccably smooth surface that space-men ran their gloved hands over in awe. Roland Barthes's essay in *Mythologies* exalts it as a cathedral on wheels: the Word made metal. In its elliptical, tubular geometry, as round as a submarine's, the DS looked as if it had been airbrushed into existence, like a photographic fantasy from the pages of *Playboy*. True, just about everything resembled a woman in some shape or form, to us, but the DS more than most: it was the mechanization of the feminine.

General de Gaulle owed his life to the DS: only a goddess, he reckoned, was capable of speeding the President away with two flat tyres after having been raked by OAS bullets. He would drive no other and was chauffeured about in a bespoke presidential limousine about twice the length of the production model, more like a steamship than a car. Vadim had one too, to supplement his fleet of Ferraris.

The driver was not Vadim, nor de Gaulle for that matter, but wore a silky white rollneck jersey aerodynamically stretched about his muscular torso. He had a tan and Ray-ban aviators and lustrous brown hair that unfurled over the shoreline of his collar. His name was René. Sinking into the upholstery, cushioned on a hydropneumatic suspension as airy and voluptuous as a hovercraft's as we floated towards Paris, Griffo let me do the talking and promptly fell asleep.

'I am not going all the way to St Tropez,' René said. 'Will Paris do?'

I said it would.

'And in St Tropez you visit Brigitte Bardot?'

How did he know? Was this a regular thing, picking up pilgrims at the side of the road? Were all hitch-hikers heading the same way? I hadn't uttered the magic word, I had vowed to keep it to myself from now on. I realized you couldn't talk about BB to just anyone. Not everyone took the subject seriously enough. But there was another reason too: call it superstition, but I knew – as I had known in the arcade at Camber Sands – that we could not show our hand too brazenly, that to admit our intentions would be fatally to frustrate them. But René, in all his DS-like omniscience, could read our minds. We didn't have to confess our dreams and desires. There was no point keeping anything from him.

'How did you know?'

'Young men go to St Tropez for one reason only.'

'So St Tropez will be teeming with fellows like us?'

'*Non, non, non.* You two, I saw it straight away, were destined for BB. She will adore you.'

René worked in film publicity and knew BB personally. 'You know she has a wonderful mind. Very intelligent. Very *spirituel.* She is the total woman. You will love her.'

There were no hills on this trip. The DS, noiseless as a flying carpet, had ironed out the bumps and bends, as if it were describing an unswerving straight line on a level plane. As we approached the *périphérique* on the northern outskirts of the capital, our journey began to seem not only feasible but as easy as jumping off a treadmill.

'Did you not ask the man for her phone number?' Griffo said after René had dropped us off. 'Ah, you eejit!'

# 18

# July 8 Continued

You say you want a revolution, well you know,
we all want to change the world.

John Lennon, 'Revolution'

Just as children used to ask, 'What did you do in the war, Daddy?' so there is now a generation in France that asks of its parents, 'What did you do in the *Evénements*?'

In 1968, after making *Shalako* with Sean Connery, and then publicizing it across the States, Brigitte Bardot returned to Paris and recorded 'Je t'aime, moi non plus' with Serge Gainsbourg. It might seem as if she was oblivious to barricades and torn-up paving stones and the dictatorship of the proletariat. While workers went on strike and the students of Vincennes charged the lines of riot police and left their blood on the boulevards, BB was breathing heavily into a microphone in a sound-proofed studio and singing, 'Viens, viens entre mes reins.'

But like Rousseau to the Revolution, BB was an inspiration to the *Evénements*. For one thing, she was doing her best to undermine capitalism and the aristocracy – as embodied by her husband, Count Gunther Sachs von Opel – from the inside, by having a string of extra-marital affairs (which was normal and tolerated by Sachs) and going noisily public about it (which wasn't). For another, she had already blazed a revolutionary trail in her films.

*Viva Maria!* (directed by Louis Malle) was made three years before 1968 and translates the pervasive metaphor of Bardot as a 'bombshell' into a plot. She plays Maria O'Reilly, explosive daughter of a French mother and an Irish Republican father who helps him as he goes about the world planting bombs. After he is killed blowing up a bridge (*à la* Roberto in *For Whom the Bell*

*Tolls*), she goes on not just to fine-tune a striptease double-act with Jeanne Moreau but also to lead an armed rebellion against some Central American junta. The lingering image (and publicity still) is less of Bardot and Moreau kicking their legs up on stage in lacey underwear than of the pair of them behind a machine gun, with Bardot pulling the trigger while Moreau puts her fingers in her ears, or Bardot skipping through a field brandishing a bomb as plump as a Christmas pudding with a lit fuse poking out of it like a sprig of holly.

*Viva Maria!* ends with all the tyrants, including the reactionary Catholic Church, being swept from power. The film is an obvious allegory of her personal struggle with General de Gaulle. But the FBI took it literally. On her 1965 American promotional tour, J. Edgar Hoover, already outraged by *And God Created Woman*, blacklisted this bleached blonde public enemy who if she could corrupt the youth of a nation could just as well destabilize the government. Sharp-suited FBI agents in France, New York and Los Angeles, like Griffo and me in Romford, diligently watched her films and spied on her movements and compiled a dossier on her background. It was the most sought-after posting in the service. Her filmic record would have made her a natural for a part in the *Godfather*: theft, mugging old ladies, drug-running, murder, suicide. And then the sequels. She had been bumped off by jealous lovers time after time, but kept on coming back for more.

In a way, Hoover was right. She was a threat to society, an extremist, a sexual subversive. J. Edgar Hoover, who frequently wore dresses in private, and Simone de Beauvoir, who wore trousers in her books, converged on this point. In 'Brigitte Bardot and the Lolita Syndrome', BB's espousal of sex is itself a politically and epistemologically loaded gesture. 'The dismantling of love and eroticism is an undertaking that can have more consequences than are imagined. As soon as a single myth is touched, all myths are in danger. A sincere gaze, however limited its range, is a fire that can set ablaze and reduce to ashes the shoddy disguises that camouflage reality.' BB was hot enough to burn down every repressive institution, not just marriage: taboos, illusions, old ideas, history, J. P. Coles (MA Cantab.), God, capital, school, virginity and grey worsted two-button suits, everything went up in smoke, vaporized by her searing, redeeming flame. It was the end of false consciousness, the beginning of the orgy.

That was the leitmotiv of the *Evénements*. Day Zero would be in May or at the latest June 1968. Of course, in reality, as opposed to Louis Malle, General de Gaulle held back the hordes with tear gas and a plebiscite before finally retiring from the field to Colombey-les-Deux-Eglises. The defining characteristic of literature, of all art, is the sense of an imminent revelation that does not occur; similarly, the *Evénements* had the sense of an imminent revolution that did not occur. But at least May 1968 had *that sense of impendingness*, the confident (if deluded) expectation of a new dawn.

Griffo and I arrived there in the second week of July. Not only had the *Evénements* missed their objective, but we had missed the *Evénements*. Back in May, preparing for my French exam, I had tuned in my transistor to the BBC reports direct from the front and listened in wonderment to the sound of the Bourse going up in flames and French civilization as we knew it being pissed down the *vespasiennes*. But when René deposited us along the Boulevard St Germain everything looked much as it had before. The barricades had gone, the workers were back at work, and the students had returned to their books. General de Gaulle was still at the Elysée and Bardot was still fellating a microphone.

Griffo was all for us heading directly to the fabled Autoroute du sud. That assembly line south would convey us straight to Lyons, and from Lyons on down to the coast. But first we had to figure out where it started. There was no mention of it on my map of the Youth Hostels of France. So we bought a map of Paris in a *papeterie*.

'Here it is,' Griffo thumbed triumphantly, 'look, the red line. It starts right here.'

'Yes, but look here. Next to the Eiffel Tower. Avenue de la Bourdonnais.'

'So?'

'Why don't we stop off there first?'

'Skip the sight-seeing – let's have the real thing.'

'It'll give us something to talk about when we meet her, evidence of good faith.'

'Talk? Who said anything about talking?'

But I had a power over Griffo I never had in England. I had been in France before and he hadn't. I knew my way around, or so he thought. I had been doing his French homework for him for years. His command of the irregular verbs was practically zero. So he more or less had to tag along. We took the Métro to Ecole militaire, sloped across a couple of streets, turning away from Les Invalides where Napoleon was entombed, and we were there: not in the street where she lived, but where she came into the world almost thirty-four years before, on 28 September 1934. It was a long, wide street, lined with cars and tall apartment blocks in brown stone and *tilleuls*.

*35 avenue de la Bourdonnais*. This biographeme had been stencilled on our brains by a hundred assorted pens. *In the shadow of the Tour Eiffel*. The theory was that the proximity of the largest erection in Paris, like a star in the ascendant, had exerted an inexorable phallocentric force over the infant Bri-Bri. Like Marcel Proust tasting a madeleine in a cup of tea, arousing men enabled her to relive her childhood memories. As we trekked past oriental carpet shops and beauty salons and the irrepressible structure leaped out at us at every intersection, the idea seemed compelling enough. Mind you, Havering Council had put up an imposing tower block at the top of Highfield Road which could be seen from all over Romford, and it had so far had little or no measurable impact on the female population.

There was the number on the wall – last stop before La Madrague. Right next door was a plaque which told of the heroism of Commandant Jean de Vogué-Vaillant and General Joinville-Malleret who 'led the national insurrection' from this very house from 19 to 25 August 1944. We too, I felt, were part of a grand revolt and were ready to sacrifice our last drop of jism in the fight.

I looked for a plaque on the wall of No. 35: *BB was born here*. And I found one: *Bibliothèque municipal*, it said. An old lady came out of the door leaning on a stick and clutching a large-print volume.

'What floor did you say it was?'

'Fifth. Take a picture – for the article.'

'It's gone. There's nothing to take a picture of. Look!'

I looked. There was no fifth floor. The building petered out after a mere two levels. I checked the number again: '35'. I ran down to the corner. 'Avenue de la Bourdonnais.' There was no mistake: we were standing in front of 35 avenue de la Bourdonnais where, every schoolboy knew – as well as he knew the longest river and the capitals of countries that now no longer exist – Brigitte Bardot had been born on the fifth floor in 1934. In vain, we surveyed the vacant space where the fifth floor should have been. There was no sign of it. A space–time lesion had opened up and swallowed it whole. Or an American collector had had it taken down brick by brick and reconstructed in Dallas.

We were not the only ones staring up at the empty sky like astronomers scanning for black holes. A few yards away stood a young woman in a navy skirt that folded across her waist, sarong-style, and white cotton shirt with a satchel looped across her chest which neatly separated and defined her small breasts. She took a book out of her bag and leafed through it, then looked up at No. 35 again, just as we had done. Then she turned and looked at us looking at her.

'*Savez-vous*,' I said, attempting my best textbook accent, '*si Brigitte Bardot est née ici*?'

She replied in English. 'I think so. Or I thought so. But where is the fifth floor? It says here,' she waved her book at us, 'she was born on the fifth floor.'

'Don't tell me you're looking for BB too?' Griffo said, with amazement.

'I am doing an assignment on Bébé. I trace her steps.'

'Are you a journalist?' I said.

'No – a student. You are journalists?'

'Yes,' I said. 'He's the photographer.'

She had cropped brown hair and looked a little like a younger Jeanne Moreau. She also looked like one of my first primary school teachers, Miss Purdie, who had returned one traumatic September as Mrs Watson. Her name was Françoise.

She suggested we ask in one of the shops. 'The Bardots lived at 34, not 35,' said a *patissière*, 'on the other side of the street.' We trooped across the avenue, and asked again to make sure. 'It was 31,' opined a man in a toy-shop. 'Opposite.' Everyone seemed to agree it was on the opposite side of the street. Except for one woman passer-by who was convinced it was not avenue de la Bourdonnais at all, but Place Violet, a few blocks away. So we went there too, but were unable to confirm the hypothesis. The evidence for her birth began to seem thin and contradictory. All we had been able to determine for sure was that she had been born in several places simultaneously, or perhaps never born at all.

The afternoon had slipped by. The sky had turned purple like cheap wine. 'Can we get going now, you bastard?' Griffo said for the tenth time, as he trailed along behind me and Françoise. 'Let her write her essay. We've got more important things to do.'

I said our good-byes.

'Where are you going?' said Françoise.

'Autoroute du sud,' said Griffo firmly.

'It's too late for that now,' she said. 'You must start first thing in the morning, when everyone is setting out. You can stay at my apartment tonight, if you want.'

Griffo thought about this for about a hundredth of a second. 'OK,' he said. 'I guess we've gone far enough for one day.'

As we headed back to Françoise's place, she stopped and gesticulated. 'You see that apartment? Third floor. That is where Bardot put her head in an oven.'

'When Vadim had that premonition? *Sacrebleu!*'

'Unless,' said Griffo, 'it was the other side of the street.'

# 19

# July 8–11

Brigitte Bardot is the main topic of conversation in 47% of all French households.

Survey in *Cinémonde*, 1963

It was not every day a woman invited us to spend the night with her. She may not have been Brigitte Bardot, but at least she definitely had an apartment in Paris – on the sixth floor. It was with a sense of mounting excitement that we approached the rue des Saints Pères in the 4è. Until, that is, Françoise said something about how delighted Roland would be to practise his English with us.

Roland was her bearded, bear-like, double-bass-playing anarchist husband, variously a Marxist, Maoist, situationist, structuralist and post-structuralist, according to mood. He was a hero of the barricades, a veteran of many a riot, she said. They were both students at the Sorbonne. Roland was getting together a band to play in a jazz concert at the Avignon Festival and they would be driving south in a few days.

'If you don't mind waiting,' Roland said, 'you can come with us.'

'We've got to hit the road,' Griffo said.

'*Tant pis.*'

'Hold on,' I said. I took Griffo on one side to consult while Françoise and Roland went into the kitchen to mull over some intractable footnote in the thoughts of Lenin or Chairman Mao while brewing coffee. 'Avignon is only a stone's throw from St Tropez. A bus-ride. We'd be there. Just one big lift and we wouldn't have to worry about hitching.'

'Might only take us a day to get down there anyway.'

'Or a week, depending.'

'If we blow it, it's your fault.'

'Don't you want to hang out with the Parisian intelligentsia?' I harboured a fantasy of us sitting in Le Flore or Les Deux Magots, knocking off philosophical tracts, *Being and Nothingness, Part II*, or another *Finnegan*, and picking up beautiful women on the strength of our brilliant ideas.

We slept on a futon, which rolled up into a sofa during the day. The walls of Françoise and Roland's bedroom were plastered with radical posters. One bore the slogan PRENEZ VOS DESIRS POUR LA REALITE ('Take your desires for reality'). Another screamed A BAS LES FLICS! I had never come across the word '*flic*', or, for that matter, the phrase '*à bas*', but the cartoon of a gendarme with an axe stuck in his head gave me the gist. It was pinned up next to a publicity poster for *Le Mépris*, in which Brigitte Bardot is leaning forwards wrapped in a towel and her breasts seem about to pop right out of the picture.

Roland and Françoise also taught us the meaning of the word *bourgeoisie* and how to pronounce it with the correct mixture of contempt and indifference. We were soon ready to toss a Molotov should the opportunity arise. One day Françoise ran a red light and was waved down by a *flic*. She opened the glove compartment. She pulled out not, as I had expected, a pistol, but her papers instead. The *motard*, looking for all the world as if he had just arrested Bonnie Parker and a couple of Clydes, gunned his bike and led us off to the commissariat. '*Il fait du zèle!*', explained Françoise.

'We've fucking had it now,' said Griffo. 'We're good and nicked.'

'What for?' I said.

'She's a terrorist and we're her sidekicks. You can kiss goodbye to Bardot.'

In the event, they fined her and let us go, having subjected us to the torture of standing in line for hours at the police station. 'How do you say, "Fair cop, guv,"' Griffo asked as we contemplated our future behind bars. As a long-time revolutionary Françoise had difficulty grasping this concept, but finally she came up with, '*Je me constitue votre prisonnier.*' This is what she would say, she said, if she had just shot her lover and she wanted to surrender to the police.

'But I would never surrender,' she added. 'I would take my own life – one bullet in his head, and one in mine.' She put a finger to my head and pulled the trigger. 'Like Bébé in *La Bride sur le cou*. With a shotgun.'

The thought of suicide was Françoise's most cherished consolation. She had tried it at least once, leaping into the Seine off the Pont des Arts – the so-called 'suicide bridge' where Bardot was often to be found, leaning over the parapet, gazing down into the dark waters, weeping. But, despite its reputation, the bridge wasn't really high enough to do any damage and Françoise had bobbed back up to the surface. When she found a glass-sided *bateau mouche* bearing down on her she had swum to the bank: it was one thing to commit suicide, another to be mowed down by a boatload of Japanese tourists.

She agreed BB had something to do with it. The head in the oven, the slashed wrists, the barbiturates. She had set a trend. 'But if I looked like Bardot,' Françoise said, 'I would not wish to commit suicide.'

'Suicide', Françoise used to say, quoting Camus, 'is the only serious philosophical problem.' As with the revolution, she took the desirability of death for granted and saw the problem in practical rather than theoretical terms, diverting us with schemes for the perfect self-murder and inviting us to chip in ideas while Roland improvised on his double-bass.

'Jump off the Eiffel Tower,' urged Griffo. Technically difficult now there was a net around the outside – and, anyway, a cliché. A good suicide was not easy. She didn't like the idea of razor blades, gas or poison. There had to be some kind of aesthetic.

'If you need an aesthetic,' Roland suggested, strumming, 'why not Jules Verne? *Tribulations d'un Chinois en Chine* – the hero pays his servant to kill him without him knowing when or where.'

'*Comme c'est beau!*' Françoise sighed.

'Then he changes his mind – but it's too late.'

Françoise took us to the Louvre and to a ping-pong match between France and China. The Chinese were the best ping-pong players in the world. Politically, they were the most advanced too. 'They are a little too thin though,' Françoise said.

'She's the one who's thin,' Griffo whispered as we lay on our futon that night. 'A regular beanpole. And a nutter.'

I fell asleep, fitfully dreaming of the intense, angst-ridden body that lay on the other side of the dividing wall, enveloped in the virile, hirsute, bomb-throwing arms of Roland, who straddled her like his bass.

Roland took us to play billiards in a hotel next to the Gare St Lazare. We couldn't get the hang of the missing pockets and only three balls. After each collision, our balls sprayed away to remote parts of the table, like pellets from a shotgun. In contrast, Roland, like a chess player, could see several moves ahead and held the balls – the two white, dotted and undotted, and a red – together in a tight triangle and generaled them around the smooth blue baize in an interlocking network of cannons, kisses and coincidences. He was not overly disappointed by the failure of the Revolution, almost the opposite. '*La lutte continue*,' he repeated with satisfaction. Roland wasn't concerned with potting the black. We asked him what it was he had been revolting against: was it Gaullism, capitalism, the class struggle? '*Non*,' he replied, 'I revolt against the lack of revolt. Against the sense that revolt is no longer possible.' And what was he revolting for? 'I revolt for the sake of revolt.'

He was supposed to be studying law, but his main job seemed to consist in subtitling Marx Brothers movies and he sought our advice on a couple of double-entendres. But often he would guillotine what he could not understand and even now the Marx Brothers appear in French cinemas overlaid with a streak of Karl Marx. Roland explained to us that *an-archos* meant 'without authority or foundation' and saw in the Marx Brothers the confirmation of his own deepest convictions. He enthused particularly over an episode in *A Day at the Races* where Groucho (Hackenbush) is going to lay a bet on Sun-Up in the 3.30 and is waylaid by Chico (Tony), pushing an ice-cream wagon ('Get your tootsie-frootsie!') as a cover for selling racing tips.

CHICHO: Pssst! You wanna something hot?
GROUCHO: Not now, I just had lunch. Anyhow, I don't like hot ice-cream.
CHICO: I no sella ice-cream. I sella tips on horses. I gotta

something can't lose. One dollar.

GROUCHO: OK. Here's a dollar.

CHICO: (*hands him an envelope*) The horse is in there.

GROUCHO: How'd he get in there? (*Reads 'ZVBXRPL'*) Hey, Ice-cream. What about this optical illusion you just slipped me? I don't understand it.

CHICO: It's in code. Look in your code-book.

GROUCHO: I haven't got any code-book.

CHICO: You no gotta code-book? I think I got one here (*fishes a book out of ice-cream wagon*).

GROUCHO: How much?

CHICO: It's free. Justa one-dollar printing charge.

GROUCHO: Hey, Ice-cream, I can't make head or tail out of this.

CHICO: You need the master code-book.

GROUCHO: Don't tell me – there's a one-dollar printing charge.

CHICO: No. Just a two-dollar delivery charge.

And so it goes on, until Groucho has bought up Chico's entire stock and Chico goes to lay the bet on Sun-Up in the 3.30 – which wins – and Groucho is left trying to sell the useless pile of books to some other poor sucker: 'Get your tutti-frutti!'

'*Tout est là!*' Roland crowed. 'Ultimate knowledge escapes us. *Nous sommes tous Groucho, n'est-ce pas?*'

'What did he say?' Griffo said.

'We're all Groucho,' I said.

'Not me, mate! I'm Chico.'

# 20

# The Night of July 11

Peuplée de cheveux longs
De grands lits et de musique
Peuple de lumière
Et peuplée de fous.

Maxime le Forestier, 'San Francisco'

(Peopled with long hair
Double beds and music
Peopled with light
And madmen and women.)

On the eve of our departure, we transferred to a house south of the boulevard Montparnasse, strategically placed for a fast getaway down the Autoroute du sud. Actually it was more an *hotel particulier* than a house, more a *château* than an *hotel*, almost a *palais*, a leafy labyrinth, an island moored in its own park in the middle of Paris. It was owned, I think, by the drummer in Roland's band.

Half of Paris was assembling there in preparation for the Avignon Festival. We sat down to a gargantuan dinner around a Rabelaisian table. Griffo and I sat side by side, Françoise sat on the other side of me and Roland was opposite. The table was so wide and the voices so loud that when they wanted to converse they had to harangue one another, as if in a disco. They shouted in French, but I remember it in English since I had to provide a simultaneous translation for Griffo. And rather like Roland, I simply cut what I didn't understand. Roland was asking Françoise about her Bardot.

ROLAND: Truth!? There is no truth!
FRANÇOISE: At least there is her point of view to take account of!

ROLAND: Don't be naive! She is a myth – a myth has no point of view!

FRANÇOISE: Simone de Beauvoir sees her as a subversive force shaking society!

ROLAND: Then Simone de Beauvoir is a fool! BB is as revolutionary as Coca-Cola! She even looks like Coca-Cola! She clothes repression with her nakedness! Her striptease is a smokescreen! Her liberation is just an adolescent delusion!

FRANÇOISE: She never sold out to Hollywood!

ROLAND: No! She is a French commodity – like Renault, sold abroad! You are a victim of advertising!

FRANÇOISE: You see her as an object! Not as subject!

ROLAND: No! I see her only at the level of ideology! She is pure connotation, not denotation, a 'signifier' as Barthes would say! Her function is to naturalize culture! Bardot is the opiate of the masses!

FRANÇOISE: I will go to St Tropez and prove she is more than a myth! You have no sympathy with the position of women!

'Fuck,' said Griffo. 'She'll completely screw us up if she tags along. Can't you say something to stop her?'

ROLAND: You are not Bardot! You are my wife! I forbid you to go to St Tropez!

FRANÇOISE: I refuse to be given orders! I will go where I please!

'No, I don't think I can,' I said.

ROLAND: *Salope!*
FRANÇOISE: *Salaud!*

Later that evening, Griffo and I were lying on a mattress on the floor upstairs. Françoise was lying on another mattress. We were sharing the same room. We could hear Roland furiously improvising down in the basement.

'Roland is very jealous, you know,' said Françoise. 'He says he will kill me if he finds me with another man. And the man too.'

'He's probably joking,' I said, uncertainly.

'Tomorrow you will find Bardot perhaps. Sometimes I think I

know her so well, I am part of her. I think she addresses me in her films. I expect her to stop in the middle of a scene and turn to the camera and say, "Hello, Françoise." I feel that close. We have so much in common, she and I.'

Françoise slid off her mattress and slid onto ours. We were lying rigidly in our shorts beneath the sheet. She was wearing a thin cotton slip. Roland's double-bass throbbed through the floorboards.

'Françoise,' Griffo said, as my hand brushed against her hip and my lips brushed her shoulder and she squirmed down between the two of us, 'you're a good Catholic. The marriage bond is sacred. You know that.'

The bass moaned up the stairs.

'Everything is permitted,' Françoise sighed. 'Sex, suicide, it has a halo over it.'

The bass bellowed. My hand touched the back of her leg. She wasn't wearing any underwear. Françoise's limbs tightened around me, like tentacles. My eyes fixed on a poster plastered to the ceiling which showed the naked top-half of a woman, with her eyes closed in pleasure and her hands on her own shadowy breasts and the words 'AAAAHHHHH!!! L'INTERNA-TIONALE SITUATIONNISTE!!!' coming out of her mouth in a bubble.

The bass expired and fell silent. As if in a mirror-version of musical chairs, Griffo leapt up, released from paralysis. 'Get outa there, you stupid arsehole,' Griffo panted, stuffing his legs into his jeans. 'He's going to rip your balls off if he finds her playing your flute.'

# July 14

VLADIMIR: Well? shall we go?
ESTRAGON: Yes, let's go. (*They do not move. Silence*).
Samuel Beckett, Waiting for Godot

Like Humphrey Bogart and his piano player, we were evacuating Paris with the sound of advancing stormtroopers in our ears, certain to be on their hit list, and we were leaving alone, men without women. But we knew that Elsa awaited us in the south.

I'll never know if Roland really would have emasculated me. We were long gone, our bags on our backs, before he came up the stairs. We had blown the lift and squandered three precious days in Paris and Griffo was pissed. I did see Françoise again after leaving school, but we fell out because I laughed at *One Flew Over the Cuckoo's Nest*, which she accused of not taking madness seriously enough. She had married Philippe, a swarthy central heating salesman from Châteauroux. Roland had qualified in law and sat as a judge in the central juvenile courts.

It being the middle of the night, we had to leg it to the Autoroute du sud. But it was worth it, we were first in line when the sun came up. The dawn driver, like Apollo in his chariot, is the most beneficent, ere traffic accumulates and tempers fray. The two *mecs* in front were rough enough to pass for bank robbers on the run or distant French cousins to the Parrish brothers, but when they said they were going to Lyons we piled in anyway. Can't judge by appearances, we said to ourselves. Still under the long shadow of Françoise, the thought passed through my sleep- and sex-starved brain that they were capable of driving to some forlorn spot, mugging us and dumping us in the back of beyond. Which is just what they did, although we were too dumb to even notice.

'Now they were the kind of blokes you know where you are with,' said Griffo, 'not like that morbid pair of yours in Paris.'

The truth was neither of us had the slightest idea where we were. Without wanting to sound too know-it-all, I had a sickly sense of foreboding. For one thing, the trip had taken about half the time I'd anticipated. For another, there was something in the way they had reacted when I burst out, 'Yippee, Lyons,' as they set us down and something in the way they had pronounced 'Lyons'. But it wasn't until I saw a signpost saying 'Orléans Centre Ville' that I was obliged to inform Griffo that we had missed our target by a matter of four letters and about four hundred miles.

'The double-crossing dagoes! Wouldn't you know it! Fucking Frenchies!'

Thus was history diverted by a *malentendu*. I was too cowardly to point out that it was really my fault. But I could have sworn the swine had said Lyons. As it was, we had fallen away from the straight and narrow and would struggle for days – years even – to get back onto it. And I joined in execrating them as loudly as anyone, as soon as I'd recovered from an afternoon's vomiting and diarrhoea, which I blamed on the bottle of milk the pirates had thrust upon us in the back of their goddam Peugeot.

Bastille Day. BB's second wedding anniversary. Sachs's too, technically, but he was out of the picture. Bardot, in short, would be needing someone to celebrate with. It was the optimal moment to descend on Marianne.

By the 14th, we were still getting occasional lifts. None of them were great lifts, the once-and-for-all lift that we dreamed of that would take us all the way there and blow away all our troubles. But we were so desperate that we had given up worrying over whether we were still going south: so long as we were going, we didn't care if it was east or west, anywhere to get us out of the immense and indeterminate centre. We drew the line at going north though. Otherwise we were blown about like autumn leaves on the unpredictable gusts of generosity. Then even those half-hearted, piddling lifts of a few kilometres this way or that dried up. We had to face it: we were becalmed in the middle of France. The centre had blown up from a dot to a diameter. The *hexagone* took on the terrifying aspect of Pascal's sphere, whose centre is everywhere and whose circumference is nowhere.

We knew that if we approached La Madrague by sea we would have to navigate around a shelf of algae which lay just beneath the surface of the water and stretched out into the bay in St Tropez. The locals called it *le mat*. Speedboats coming to spy on BB on the beach regularly got stuck in it and had to be cut out. Nature had thrown a cordon sanitaire around her, protecting the pearl with hidden traps. St Tropez was a Bermuda triangle, a Sargasso Sea of shipwrecked sailors looking for anchorage in BB's cove. Even a helicopter pilot, circling around the naked sunbather, had ventured too low and been sucked down into the depths. But we were wise to these hazards and eschewed the use of speedboats and helicopters. What we hadn't known was that *le mat* extended hundreds of miles inland and covered the approach by road as well.

We found ourselves outside a city called Nevers according to the sign. We took shelter under a tree with no leaves, and jerked our thumbs out sporadically. 'We'll Nevers get out of here,' Griffo cracked.

'Nev-*air*,' I corrected him. But, nuances of pronunciation aside, he was right. We were so far beyond even the expectation of a lift that we had attained a state of philosophical resignation and could barely summon the interest or the energy to spit at the few cars that went speeding by. We squatted down on a hunk of dirt at the side of the road, tormented by heat and thirst and shimmering oases.

'Hey, look at this one,' Griffo yelled in my ear, yanking my arm and dragging me to my feet. 'It's British!'

It was a slow-moving vehicle: an old Ford Consul with GB plates and a trailer hitched to the rear. Inside were two red-haired girls. They weren't driving, they were passengers in the back seat: their parents were doing the driving. As they drew level, we had plenty of time – more than a second – to absorb quite how breathtakingly beautiful they were, not to mention how sympathetic and tender.

We proposed to them with our thumbs, pleaded with our eyes. Yes, we said with complete sincerity, we are ready to sacrifice our lives to you if you will only give us a lift. 'We're British!' we screamed out, on the assumption that they would not marry foreigners. We spared a fraction of a second to look ourselves over with the harsh and objective gaze of the Other: dusty, yes, but not dirty; bedraggled, certainly, but not without a remnant of charm beneath the rags.

As we clapped eyes on their eyes, we knew it was love at first sight on their side too. Now the Consul was passing and there was, as yet, no sign of it slowing down. Inside the car, however, there were signs of frantic activity. The two girls were leaning forwards and tapping the driver on the shoulder, 'Dad! You've got to stop and give those two handsome boys a lift. There's lots of room.' The driver looked in his mirror and inspected his daughter's suitors. For a fleeting instant, the Consul seemed to slow and our hearts sped up. Then the Consul jammed down the throttle and kept on going, the two girls in the back window blew us kisses and threw up their hands and vanished into the dust, and we sank down despondent on the dirt once more.

We had our heads buried deep in our hands when we heard the two harmonious voices chiming in our ears. 'Well, don't just sit there,' they said. 'Hop in!' The red-haired girls were identical twins with freckles and come-with-us smiles and bright green eyes.

We were saved. The Consul had changed its mind and reversed back to us. We leapt to our feet and charged up to the car. Their parents were grinning hugely. 'You thought for a moment we weren't going to stop, didn't you?' laughed the driver. His wife laughed a merry laugh and we joined in the laughter. It had been a good joke and now our suffering was over and we could give vent to our relief, loudly, uproariously. It was only fair that we should have to suffer before attaining our goal; but it was equally fair that, having suffered, we should attain it and not just go on suffering for no good reason, innocent and deserving cases as we were.

We started trying to cram ourselves and our packs into the back of the Consul. 'You're not all going to fit in here,' pointed out the driver. 'You'd better put yourselves in the van. Milly, get them settled, will you?'

The girls' mother bade us sink down in padded sofas that jutted out from the wall. 'Now you're not really supposed to be in here while we're on the road, but,' she winked benevolently, 'sit quietly and you'll be fine and no one need ever know.'

She went to close the door, but Alice and Lucy – such were the names of the redheads – protested. 'Mum, Mum, can we sit in the caravan too? It's so much more fun than the back of the car.'

Milly gazed at them sceptically. 'But, girls, what will your father say?'

'Please, Mum, please!' they begged.

'Oh, all right then,' their mother smiled. 'But sit nicely and don't get into trouble. I'll tell your father you're keeping an eye on the boys.'

We were already necking before the Consul had started up again. As it cruised south, so too did we, kissing their freckled breasts and working our way down to the earthy Midi of their unbelievable bodies. By a stroke of good fortune, the Consul was going all the way to St Tropez. We hooted as we looked out of the window from time to time and saw that many of the pitiless vehicles that had passed us by had broken down and were marooned with their bonnets in the air or lay smashed at the bottom of jagged ravines. It was not long before we were pulling into the dreamy fishing village on the Riviera.

Alice and Lucy beseeched us to come to the caravan site on the hill and stay with them there, but Griffo and I stood firm. We had a date with destiny on the beach. They would wait for us, they promised, and we promised we would return to them as soon as we could. The Consul drove up the hill and we walked down the hill.

We ran rejoicing into the cobalt sea, and the soft sun towelled us down as we stretched out on the sand in our trunks. In no time, a shadow passed before us, blotting out the sun. We screwed open our eyes. There was no mistaking BB. She towered over us, monumental, monolithic, flawless, glistening, a cheetah panting on a leash by her side, her breasts and thighs pulling impatiently at the strings of her totally inadequate bikini.

*Don't blow it now!* we said telepathically to one another. *Stay cool!* We stayed cool. This was the day, the hour, the moment, we had been building up to all our short lives, and we weren't going to blow it. We lay there, being grilled beneath the toaster of BB's gaze.

'*Venez,*' she said. She led us to her white Rolls Royce, parked beside the beach, where her ebony-black chauffeur waited imperturbably. As we advanced upon the heavy green gates of La Madrague, emblazoned with the entwined initials BB, we could dimly make out the dozens of supplicants pressed up against the unyielding ironwork, reaching through the bars, crying out unintelligibly. Some resembled us, others had grown old in their vigil, some no longer moved. Silently, the gates swung open before us, but only for us, and clanged shut on the wretched multitude as we swept up to the simple Provençal house where fountains played and animals roamed along an avenue fanned by whispering palm trees and tall beach grass.

A banquet lay prepared for us on the rough-hewn mahogany refectory table, of passion fruit and pineapples and melons and bananas and long, long baguettes. When we were satisfied and could eat no more, BB took us by the hand and led us to her boudoir.

In a trice we were naked. A filter threw a crimson light over us.

BB: Do you find my feet pretty?
A&G: Yes.
BB: And my ankles – you like them?
A&G: Oh yes.
BB: You like my knees too?
A&G: Yes, I love your knees.
BB: And my thighs?
A&G: And your thighs.
BB: You see my backside in the mirror?
A&G: Yes.
BB: Do you find my buttocks lovely?
A&G: Yes . . . very.
BB: And my breasts, you like them?
A&G: Yes, enormously. (*They try to embrace them.*)
BB: *Doucement!*
A&G: Sorry!

The filter changed from red to white and then blue.

BB: Which do you prefer: my breasts or my nipples?
A&G: Must we choose?
BB: And my shoulders, what do you think?

A&G: Beautiful.
BB: I feel they are not quite rounded enough. My arms?
A&G: Perfection.
BB: My face?
A&G: The same.
BB: Everything? Mouth, eyes, nose, ears?
A&G: Everything.
BB: Then you love me totally?
A&G: Totally, tenderly, tragically.

She plunged back on the bed and pulled us onto her and into her, and made us slaves to her every desire. She was as deep as the sea and we could never get to the bottom of her.

'Enough! enough!' we whimpered.

'*Encore, encore,*' she retorted, insatiably.

In the midst of our writhings, my head must have jerked from my hands, where it had been cradled, because I awoke from this exquisite, intolerable day-dream with a start beneath the shrivelled leafless tree on the road out of Nevers. The Consul was nowhere in sight. The red-haired girls had gone from our lives. Only BB remained, for better for worse, for richer for poorer, in sickness and in health, till death us do part, our constant mirage of a companion.

## 22

# That Night

JOURNALIST: What was the best day of your life?
BARDOT: It was a night.

Press conference, 1956

There were no cars, none, nowhere, evening was drawing on, and there was nothing for it but to hoof it back to town in search of a bed for the night. Two geezers not much older than us walked by as we gazed pointlessly at my map. 'What are you looking for?' one of them said in French.

I constructed one of my best sentences. 'We were hoping to find the *auberge de la jeunesse.*'

'The *what*?'

'The *auberge de la jeunesse*,' I repeated loudly.

'What is he saying?' said one to the other.

'*Au-berge de la jeune-esse*,' I spelt out laboriously.

They gave me blank looks.

'My God, can you not understand French?' I moaned.

'You are English, no?'

'Yes.'

'Let us speak English. What is it you want?

'The youth hostel.'

'Ah! the *auberge de la jeunesse*. Why did you not say this?'

'Can you tell us where it is?' I gritted my teeth.

'There is no youth hostel,' he said.

'Thanks,' I said, with all the bitterness I could muster.

'Is there anywhere else – cheap – to stay?' Griffo chipped in.

'There is a *camping* one or two kilometres along this road,' said the other bloke, and waved in the direction of Nevers.

'We have no tents,' I said.

'They have a *dortoir*,' he said.

The two kilometres turned to ten as we humped the hundred-weight sacks of coal on our backs under the light of the moon, pondering the fundamental question of whether it had really been necessary to include the Jaeger jumper and the waiter's jacket.

We passed a smattering of petrol stations and a Mammouth *hypermarché*. Le Camping de Nevers was on the edge of town, along an unmade track. We cheered up as the bright lights of the main reception building led us manfully past the massed ranks of GB-plated caravans, presumably lured there by the French Tourist Office who put out an ad in the *Daily Mail* on 13 July: 'France is ready to welcome you . . . For next to nothing you can stay on French camping sites with excellent facilities.'

'Caravans!' Griffo snorted.

'Tents!' I sneered. 'Who needs 'em?'

There was a sign in the window of the camping office: 'COMPLET'. We stared soulfully through the glass door, but the man behind the counter shut us out with his arms.

We sat down on our rucks on the verandah outside.

'Do you think we should start looking for a hotel?' I said.

'Nah!' said Griffo. 'Let's just kip on one of the benches. We'll rough it.'

I remembered the phrase for camping out: *passer la nuit à la belle étoile*. It conferred an irresistible glamour on the business of sleeping rough. I looked up at the speckled navy blue sky. This was living. This was what we had come here for.

'Better than the hostel,' Griffo enthused. 'No smelly feet up your nose. Fresh air in your lungs. And all for free. What could be finer?'

We lay down on a couple of adjacent wooden benches, our heads propped up on our packs, folded our arms and settled down comfortably for the night. We hadn't eaten for hours, but it didn't matter. We were hungry but happy. It must have been about one o'clock and I was sleeping soundly when Griffo tapped me awake. 'I'm cold,' he said. 'Aren't you?'

I dug out the Jaeger, the jade green crew-neck with the ribbing, vindicated after all, and passed it to him. We wrestled with our benches for a while. Then it started to rain. First lightly, then heavily. Our first thought was to sneak into reception and shelter there, but it was locked. Only one door was open and that we went through – into the men's toilets, a squat brick building with a cement floor, a urinal along one wall and a handful of cubicles opposite with holes in the floor.

We piled in out of the rain and perched on our packs, listening to the pounding on the roof. There was a light that switched off automatically after a minute. We got up every minute to switch it back on for fear that someone would stumble over us in the darkness. The rain continued its steady static. Even so we would look outside every now and then for a sign of it coming to an end.

'Even if it stops everything'll be soaked,' Griffo said. 'We'll have to hole up here.'

'You mean *sleep* here?'

'Look on the bright side,' he said. 'It's handy if you want to take a leak.' He sniffed cautiously. 'The pong's not too bad either.'

'Remember when BB is touching up her lipstick in *And God Created Woman* and listening in to the conversation in the gents?'

'Yeah.'

'And she hears Antoine saying he's only after a one-night stand and no way he's going to take her to Toulon.'

'I'd take her to Toulon. Why don't you pop next door and ask her?'

We stretched out against the unoccupied wall, in the hope of not being pissed on during the night. We had but one sleeping bag between the two of us, and that was just a sheet envelope, designed to fit onto youth hostel mattresses. Technically, it was mine, since Griffo had counted on being able to hire them out in every hostel we stayed at. But – *noblesse oblige* – I went along with his plan to toss for it. It was only big enough for one. There wasn't a chance of sharing.

'Tails,' I called.

'Son-of-a-bitch bastard fucking cunt!' he said, sliding his hand off the coin.

I hunched up inside the sheet and turned my face to the wall and shut my eyes. The urinal flushed itself and dripped a while. Someone lurched into the toilet and switched the light on. '*Ouf, pardon!*'

'*Je vous en prie*,' I said.

He relieved himself quietly and tiptoed out.

Five minutes.

'D'you think we could do shifts with the sleeping bag?'

'OK,' I said. 'One hour in, one hour out. All right? Wake me up in an hour.'

Another five minutes.

'D'you think there's room for two in that bag?'

'No.'

'Jesus, man, you selfish sod, you'd let your own mother freeze to death in front of you, you would.'

'All right, all right, you have the first hour.'

I started unpeeling the bag. Griffo held me back. 'You don't have to get out. There's plenty of room in there. Just squeeze up a bit, will you.'

'Take your boots off at least.'

He squashed in beside me, splitting the seams at the top. We were packed as tight as two arms in the same sleeve. It was physically impossible to fit back to back, so Griffo wriggled about and slotted himself behind me, with both of us on our sides and his arms around my shoulders.

'Just don't get an erection, for God's sake,' I prayed.

'Ah, *mon chéri*,' he sighed.

'Do you think we could get some sleep now?'

The light flicked on again. '*Ouf! Pardon!*' Then the sound of discreet, retreating steps. The bladder could wait. He wasn't going to unzip his flies with a couple of inverts lying in ambush in a bag.

After a couple of weeks in France we had finally found somebody to go to bed with.

## PART THREE
# Betrayal

Car ce que nous croyons notre amour, notre jalousie, n'est pas une même passion continue, indivisible. Ils se composent d'une infinité d'amours successifs, de jalousies différentes et qui sont éphémères, mais par leur multitude ininterrompue donnent l'impression de la continuité, de l'unité.

Proust, *Du côté de chez Swann*

(For what we suppose to be our love, our jealousy, are, neither of them, single, continuous and indivisible passions. They are composed of an infinity of successive loves, of different jealousies, each of which is ephemeral, although by their uninterrupted multitude they give us the impression of continuity, the illusion of unity.)

# 23

# July 1972

> Le supplément est toujours le supplément d'un
> supplément. On veut remonter du supplément à la
> source: on doit reconnaître qu'il y a du supplément à la
> source.
>
> Jacques Derrida, De la grammatologie

> (The supplement is always the supplement of a
> supplement. We want to get back from the supplement
> to the source, but we are forced to recognize that the
> supplement is at the source too.)

Four years later I checked into a hotel in St Tropez. I had missed
my deadline for the *Romford Recorder*. It took me exactly three
years longer to reach the south of France than it had taken to
land a man on the moon.

I went the long way round from Nevers: via Paris and
England. In July 68, like Apollo 8 in December, like Jules Verne's
Barbicane et al. in 1868, we had only orbited our target and then
hurtled back to earth without touching down at Tranquillity
Base. It was Griffo's idea to pull out. I could have gone on hoping
and dreaming and going round in circles a lot longer – I still am.
But Griffo was more pissed off than I was after that night on the
toilet floor. We were never going to make it down to fucking St
Tropez. We'd be better off back in Romford. At least there were
johns with seats there and beds.

Vadim's account of his split with Bardot applied *mutatis
mutandis* to Griffo and me:

> The two people find themselves alone, driven by obscure
> desires and lost dreams. I see passion as a boat in which two
> people play and make love without noticing in their carefree

happiness that there is a hole in the bottom. Their eyes are turned towards their destination, a beach holding out the promise of hot, white sand and shady trees. Day after day, week after week, the boat draws nearer the shore where they will live happily ever after, safe from the uncertainties of sea and weather. But the boat usually sinks before they reach the shore.

That summer there were simultaneous sightings of BB in St Tropez, Italy (where she rented Gina Lollobrigida's villa outside Rome) and England. I still half expect to come across a cutting, dated some time in the middle of July '68 and bearing the headline 'BB, ES-SEX KITTEN?':

On her whistle-stop tour of Europe, Brigitte Bardot yesterday stopped off in Romford. Asked why she had come to this goddess-forsaken place, she said she was looking for a fifteen-year-old English boy to co-star in her next film, to be entitled *The Road to St Tropez*. 'Or better still, two of them.' Pressed as to whether it was probable or indeed inevitable that her co-stars would ultimately become her lovers, she said, 'All things are possible. But I try never to think of the future.' Many fifteen-year-old boys stepped forward to volunteer. But she found no one to meet her requirements and left to continue her quest elsewhere.

In the end, she ditched millionaire nightclub owner Luigi Rizzi and settled on Patrick Gilles, a 23–year-old leather-jacketed student from St-Etienne, who would graduate with a part in her next film, the Franco-Italian production *Les Femmes*, and make a series of cameo appearances in newsreels around the world as her current bedfellow.

Griffo, who blamed our failure on me, went to Scarborough with Kevin Nichol. They went by train. Kevin Nichol – a trainee photographer who was as knowledgeable as a gynaecologist and whose room was papered with nudes – was to be his lucky charm. In Scarborough they wound up with more girls than they could handle. 'They were coming out of our ears!' Griffo crowed later. 'They were coming out of the walls!'. One of them eventually became his wife.

I read that Brigitte Bardot moved Patrick Gilles into La Madrague, then took off to the Bahamas with him, renting a bungalow on Naked Island.

I struck back by going out with a librarian called Wendy from Hornchurch branch library. I hung around until closing time one Saturday and invited her to a party at Geoff Russell's place. Griffo was there. I hadn't seen him for the best part of a year and he boasted to me about Scarborough. I remember that Wendy used the word 'stultifying', which at the time I didn't really understand, but I nodded my head in agreement all the same.

Perhaps it was that same night, in the dying embers of the decade, as the shades of the seventies began to close upon the growing boy, that I had sex for the first time in Wendy's parents' house while her parents were away. I'm not sure. I wasn't sure then. She was gorgeous, she was brainy, she was writing a novel in French (easier, she said, than writing in English because you didn't have so many words to choose between). I was looking forward to the memorable and metamorphic moment in which I would at last attain orgasm *inside a girl*. '*Je viens, je viens entre tes reins.*' But somehow it slipped by me unrecorded.

'Did anything happen?' I said.

'Of course,' she said.

'Oh,' I said. 'Great.'

My sexual initiation, so long beckoning from the future, had sailed straight by me and on into the past without ever pausing in the present. The subject of so much anticipation had instantly become an object of nostalgia. The central experience had eluded me and I would have to reconstruct it on the basis of educated guesses and hearsay. My foundations, like John Griffin's, were largely imaginary.

Wendy had hopes of becoming a call-girl, but the last I heard she was studying art history at Essex. I became doggedly devoted to her and she went off with a welder from Bristol. Griffo set up in building with John, Brigitte Bardot made *Les Femmes* and I put off university to go back to France. If Griffo blamed me then I certainly blamed him. This time I would go it alone. Unable to bear the prospect of hitch-hiking and too broke to afford the train, I decided to cycle to St Tropez, inspired by watching the Tour de France on television, buoyed by the knowledge of Sachs's marriage to Marianne Inger Larssen in St Moritz where the couple left the wedding in a bobsleigh, and undeterred by word that Bardot had taken up with – in no particular order – an actor from the Comédie Française, a publisher and a shipping tycoon.

The bike was metallic blue with drop-handlebars and panniers, and it was the panniers that did for me. They snapped back and bit my hand when I unhooked them from the frame, they dragged me and the bike backwards even on the flat. Only there was no flat, just an unmapped mountain range between Boulogne and Paris. Whatever direction I rode in, the wind was against me, and if I turned round the wind would wheel right round with me. I took the weight off my pedals by latching on to the back of a Chambourcy van on the outskirts of Paris which nearly ripped my arm off. Finally I stuffed a brick in the panniers and drowned them, bought a rucksack and went back to hitching. At least I didn't have Griffo on my back as well.

When I say 'checked into a hotel', I should add 'only when no one was looking'. I got a lift to Avignon, caught the bus and arrived in St Tropez about 1 am. I had the beach to myself and curled up happily on a deckchair: it was a cold night and I could have done with an overcoat, but I was sustained by the knowledge that BB was close by.

It must have been about 3 am that the gendarme joined me. My conversation at 3 am is limited at the best of times. This was not the best of times. The gendarme had all the lines. '*C'est rigoureusement interdit!* (It is strictly forbidden)' was one of them. '*Cette plage est privée* (this is a private beach),' was another.

I opened my mouth to say, 'The beach, monsieur, is the last refuge of *liberté, égalité, fraternité*. It belongs to everyone and no one. The beach is for *being*, not *having*. The beach is where primeval fish first dragged themselves up out of the water to evolve into mankind and where we therefore return to rediscover our origins. The beach is where we come to escape rules and regulations and strip off the laws of society. The beach is where we come to find ourselves and meet our destiny. The beach is a *coincidentia oppositorum*, where the land and the sea contend, where water, earth, fire and air are melded in alchemical union. The beach is the borderline between the conscious and the unconscious. The beach is where we see children sport upon the shore and hear the mighty waters rolling evermore. Bougainville, Gauguin, Jack London, all found solace or salvation on the beach. If there is a world in a grain of sand then there is a whole universe on the beach. The beach is reality rolled up in a towel. The beach is sex. The beach is truth.' No one was ever tossed off a beach in the sixties, I was sure. But I was tired, it was the seventies, and I could tell this was the kind of gendarme who would have banished Jesus from the beach on the Sea of Galilee, so all I said was, *'D'accord,'* picked up my bag and vamoosed.

I selected my establishment with care, steering clear of the ultra-flashy pleasure-domes with flunkies still manning the doors, and the modest pensions which had already locked theirs, and homing in on a salubrious four-star with a revolving door and an unoccupied foyer. I flopped down on the nearest available armchair. I was kicked out around six, protesting that I had come to book in and, no, I had not seen the COMPLET sign, but if they were going to be like that about it then they could – I span out of the door – *aller au diable*. It was an archaic and feeble malediction, but my French wasn't good enough to be properly insulting.

Obviously the bus-driver had made an error. I had paid to go to heaven and he had dropped me off in hell. And still it was packed. I scoured town for a bed for the night, but I might as well have been thumbing a lift in Nevers. I hate it when you go into a hotel and ask for a room and the hotelier laughs mirthlessly in your face. *'Vous auriez une chambre, Monsieur, pour une seule personne?'* 'Ho ho ho ho ho ho ho ho!' You'd think I'd been asking for a room with BB. I searched for La Madrague but found only the zillionaire yachts in the harbour. Too poor for a guidebook, I was too embarrassed to ask for directions: everyone already knew which house it was, everyone except me. La Madrague was the unofficial Eiffel Tower of St Tropez and I couldn't see it. I collapsed on the beach for a spell in the afternoon, but it was crowded and hot and naked, scented with the aroma of roasting flesh, and the wind whipped sand in my eyes and I was nervous of gendarmes and deckchair-ticket collectors and thieves. That evening, reluctantly following in the footsteps of Antoine in *And God Created Woman*, I caught the bus out of town to Toulon, where Napoleon had embarked on his magnificent and futile Egyptian campaign.

Like the French army at St Jean D'Acre, I had besieged St Tropez and been repulsed. The difference was that I didn't return to become Emperor. But if I wasn't claiming victory, I wasn't going to admit defeat either.

Perhaps St Tropez had once been a sleepy fishing village. Certainly it was one no longer. There was a rumour that Brigitte Bardot was no longer BB, even supposing she ever had been. In 1958, shortly after seeing *En cas de malheur*, in which BB persuades an ageing Jean Gabin, playing a Parisian lawyer, to take her case by lifting her dress to reveal that she is wearing no underwear, Marguerite Duras wrote an idyllic essay in the *Nouvel Observateur*, in which she argues that 'La reine Bardot' coincides perfectly with her own character: there was no distinction between Brigitte Bardot and BB and both were beacons of bad behaviour, the irresistible threat to every marriage. Just six years later, she had changed her tune. BB, now aged thirty, was perceptibly in decline.

> Certainly her body, though a trifle less well moulded inside her golden skin, still remains superb. But in her face something has frozen. A slight puckering of the mouth and the eyes, which yesterday was not there. Yesterday, facing the world, this face was majestically carefree. Today she keeps a close watch on it. That is the difference – her pose. In other words, fear. Is this the end of a dazzling morning? Of course not – but already the warning signs of evening are here. An evening full of wolves.

And that was in 1964, four years before Griffo and I first took to the road. Actually disillusion had already set in at exactly the same time as illusion, or possibly even before. In 1958 the *Daily Herald* was gloatingly rubbing its hands and predicting, 'In two years she will be just another continental bosom and wiggle girl. In five years people will be saying: Brigitte Bardot? Oh yes, she was that French girl they used to make all the fuss about!' We were not voyeurs so much as vultures, impatient to swoop and pounce, alert for the least sign of a crack or flaw. But the first crack was not in the body of Bardot but her mind.

Duras argued that BB's liaisons were born of desperation,

fuelled by an unquenchable need to fill the void. She took lovers because she was lonely, but she was lonely because she didn't even have herself. If Roger Vadim could possess her only in the eyes of others, so too she felt she truly existed only in the form of an object of desire. 'The sleep of her lover is her sleep. I don't say that this is selfishness, no. I'm saying something quite different – that Bardot is a mythological being even in her own eyes.'

But in this Bardot is not alone, since existing and acting are two and the same. In a famous passage in *Being and Nothingness*, Sartre writes of the garçon in a café that:

> He has lively and emphatic gestures, a little too precise, a little too swift, he approaches his customers with a step a little too rapid, he bends over with a little too much eagerness, his voice, his eyes express an overly solicitous interest in the customer's order, and he returns attempting to imitate in his gait the inflexible rigour of some automaton, carrying his tray with all the temerity of a tightrope walker . . . All his behaviour seems to us like a game.

What is he doing? He is 'playing at being a *garçon de café*'.

The garçon is held up as a primary case of 'bad faith' – falsely assuming an identity in contravention of the law of freedom. But the phenomenon of bad faith is so cogently articulated, so instantly recognizable, that its opposite, *authenticity*, seems a shadow, a ghost, a mere hypothesis. If Sartre was right that 'man is what he is not and is not what he is,' and Popeye was wrong in naively asserting that 'I am what I am and that's all that I am,' then everyone must be guilty of bad faith. How could Brigitte Bardot not play at being BB, whose role was not to play a role? She was simply better at it than all the other women who also played at being BB.

Her affirmation of individuality, applauded by Beauvoir, is denounced by Duras as a hoax. Bardot, in the early sixties, bestrode a faultline in intellectual history. She was the personification of a rift in the *epistēmē*. It was as if, in the very lines of her body, Sartre could be seen to shade into Lévi-Strauss and Barthes, permissive phenomenology chastened by the rigours of morphology and mythology. Bardot dramatized the sense of necessity already buried within the concept of freedom. In

Beauvoir she was a heroine of liberation; in Duras she has become its victim. She was being romanced all over again, once more grasped as an exemplary figure, but this time around precisely because we are all in some way subject to determinism: 'One day,' Duras concluded, 'she will discover that what is happening to her is neither more nor less than the fate of all human beings and nothing else.'

In *Masculin-féminin* (Godard, 1965, in which she appears for just eighty-five seconds), when one of the other characters spots her in a bar he says, 'She looks exactly like Brigitte Bardot.' But always she must have doubted her credibility in the part and would have been tempted to overcompensate accordingly. In *Viva Maria!*, in *Babette s'en va-t-en guerre*, in *La Bride sur le cou*, she would exhibit lively and emphatic gestures, a little too precise, a little too swift, she would approach with a step a little too rapid, bend over with a little too much eagerness, her voice, her eyes expressing an overly solicitous interest in the customer's order. She too would, at times, imitate the inflexible rigour of an automaton, the temerity of a tightrope walker. When she was at her most real she was acting; but when she acted she became unreal.

Borges, in his essay 'Borges and I', maintains that we are all monstrously two-fold: 'I like hourglasses, maps, eighteenth-century typography, the taste of coffee and the prose of Stevenson; he shares these preferences, but in a vain way that turns them into the attributes of an actor. It would be an exaggeration to say that ours is a hostile relationship; I live, let myself go on living, so that Borges may contrive his literature.' In the same way BB justifies Bardot, but also haunts and torments her. Borges writes that he tried without success to free himself from Borges. It is easy to imagine Bardot uttering Borges's sentence, 'My life is a flight.' In 1959 Beauvoir linked her with James Dean and discerned in her a comparable 'tragic intensity – the fever of living, the passion for the absolute, the sense of the imminence of death.' Bardot made her second suicide attempt in 1960.

Immediately after celebrating her twenty-sixth birthday she took an overdose of barbiturates and slashed her wrists. She had just finished making *La Vérité* with Henri-Georges Clouzot, a sort of *L'Etrangère* in which Bardot enjoys casual sex, accidentally bumps off her lover and finds her life-style on trial, slashing her wrists before the jury can reach a verdict. To Clouzot, during her birthday lunch at the Colombe d'Or, Bardot had said: 'I have no private life any more. I have no life to speak of at all. I am a hunted woman. I can't take a step without being surrounded and questioned. I am being tortured. I would so much like to be a woman just like everyone else.' She had already broadcast the news on television: 'I want to say: BB is no more. Long live Brigitte!' Her suicide note (some say there was no note) strikes an over-confident note: 'I am going to change things one way or another.'

But death and authenticity continued to elude her. It was as if the more she tried to get away from BB, the more she was being BB. There was no escape. The *News Chronicle* put the 'suicide' in quotation marks and dismissed it as 'a new gimmick to get Bardot back on Page One.' Her career was on the slide and the only way out was to re-enact a scene from *La Vérité*. The Truth was a lie. Her entire life and her death, in short, were nothing other than a fake, a scriptwriter's yarn, a post-Vadim PR scam.

Sceptics heaped scorn, but so did the believers. From a Catholic point of view, it was a case of yet another commandment being violated: first she betrays the family, then she betrays the sacred gift of life itself. I remember that newspapers were covertly sympathetic to the first woman to see Bardot after her suicide manqué – all bandages and dark glasses in a hospital lift – who tried to stab her in the face with a fork: they tended to agree that it was an outrage that she, Bardot, should be so heedless of life when the woman's son, a soldier, had been killed fighting for his country. They wanted to stab her too.

I feel a twinge of guilt on account of her suicide bid. I feel as if I drove her to it, even though I was only seven or eight at the time and had yet to meet her at Camber Sands. After all, I was, in my small way, responsible for the persistence of BB. 'If only every man who sees my films did not get the impression he can make love to me, I would be a lot happier.' But the same applied to her husbands: if only every man who marries me did not get the impression he can possess me. In any case, I was not *every man*. I was me – or part of me was, just as part of Brigitte Bardot really was BB. We have had a tempestuous relationship, she and I, the kind that often ends in melodrama, although – God knows – I had more justification for barbiturates and razor blades than she did.

# 24

# 1974–75

Puisque je suis coupable de ceci, de cela (j'ai, je me
donne mille raisons de l'être), je vais me punir, je vais
abîmer mon corps: me faire tailler les cheveux très
court, cacher mon regard derrière des lunettes noires
(façon d'entrer au couvent), m'adonner à l'étude d'une
science sérieuse et abstraite. Je vais me lever tôt pour
travailler pendant qu'il fait encore nuit, tel un moine.

Roland Barthes, *Fragments d'un discours amoureux*

(Since I am guilty of this, of that (I have, I invent, a
thousand reasons for being so), I shall punish myself, I
shall chasten my body: cut my hair very short, conceal
my eyes behind dark glasses (a way of taking the veil),
devote myself to the study of some serious and abstract
branch of learning. I shall get up early and work while
it is still dark outside, like a monk.)

My passion for BB cooled a few degrees after the St Tropez
fiasco. I blamed Bardot for the gendarme, the yachts and the hot-
dog stands. It was all her fault that the fishing village and resort
of painters and intellectuals had turned into another chapter on
the overdevelopment and corruption of the Riviera. She it was
who had put the *trop* into St Tropez. I would have nothing more
to do with her. Fuck you, Brigitte!

St Tropez, like the moon, was just a handful of dust, a hunk of
rock, bereft of life, worthless, barren, mindless. Instead of
shooting for the stars, NASA backtracked, insolvent and
unloved, its great Niagara of funding dried to a trickle, its rocket
fuel of dreams all burned up and spent. Abjuring the sinful
pleasures of the world, I resolved to dedicate myself to higher
things, the life of the mind, a world of pure ideas, and took my
vows at Sussex University in Brighton, where I majored in

French. It was not only BB and St Tropez I was relinquishing for all time: it was Griffo and Romford. But if I gave up pursuing her, she in revenge, under cover of a succession of alter egos, began pursuing me. Brighton, on the south coast of England, would come to seem like St Tropez with pebbles. Even the first four letters of the town called out her name.

In 1973, with Britain at last a timorous, quivering member of the EEC, BB chose this moment to exercise her veto. The twilight of the idol had finally set in. After making *L'Histoire très bonne et très joyeuse de Colinot Trousse-Chemise* (*The Edifying and Joyous story of Colinot, the Skirt Puller-Upper*), which was neither *très bonne* nor *très joyeuse*, Bardot was offered the lead in a film called *Someone is Killing the Great Chefs of Europe*. She turned it down on the grounds that the titles of her films were getting longer than her own part in them, surrendering the role to Jacqueline Bisset, as if handing on the baton of responsibility for the sexual fantasies of a generation.

In retirement she consistently rubbished her own movies. She had made, by her own reckoning, no more than three good ones or possibly only one or possibly none. But then she had always been detached from her career, her public persona. 'I can be replaced tomorrow by somebody else with the same set of dimensions. I don't care. It's all a fairy tale, and like a fairy tale, it will probably have an ending. I only hope it's a happy one.' She was a Cinderella in reverse: the rich girl who went to the ball and jilted the prince.

'The myth of BB is finished,' BB announced in 1974, on her fortieth birthday. 'Perhaps in five years people will have forgotten me, maybe not. I will be forty-five. I'll be able to live like everyone else . . . I will no longer be a beautiful object but a human being.' The gap between Bardot and BB, as between me and BB, was steadily increasing. Both of us needed something else to do.

In the summer of 1975, as Pilou lay dying, I fell in love and Brigitte Bardot set her heart on saving the baby seals of Newfoundland. Most people make the mistake of seeing a schism between her film career and the BB Wildlife Foundation. They distinguish between two quite distinct Bardots, or two incarnations of the same woman, as if she had been reborn as a believer in something completely different. But there is a natural continuum between the successive phases of her life.

One of her pet spaniels (Clown) had a walk-on part in *And God Created Woman*. Gunther Sachs briefly regained her affection by buying her a pet cheetah. When she divorced Sachs in 1969 she turned for consolation to her donkey, Cornichoo, and a red setter called Patapon. It was said she preferred animals to human beings, that she had turned her back on mankind at large. Having made a poor job of motherhood, dumping her only child (Nicolas Charrier) on her husband and then dumping her husband, she adopted a series of surrogate children – dogs, parrots, horses. Simone de Beauvoir was wrong to see the love of animals ascribed to Bardot as some kind of PR trick, designed to appeal to the pastoral side of the French character, to soften her image and make her more publicly digestible. Her devotion to animals was perfectly genuine, while the gastronomic French public cared little except for their taste. So it was that when she pulled out of acting, birds and beasts would move in to fill the bedspace vacated by droves of auditioning lovers.

There is speculation among Bardot-watchers that she identified with animals because she saw herself as an endangered species, prey to photographers and producers and directors. She appeared in at least three films (*La Vie privée*, *Paparazzi*, *Tentazione proibite*) which depict her as a martyr to celluloid fame, reified, commodified, persecuted, movies that advertise her very public demand for obscurity. In a way, all her films lepidopterized her career, her character: every lens was a butterfly net, a pin and a glass case. 'Whenever I am being photographed,' she is supposed to have said, 'I know what it is like to be a wild animal caught in the telescopic sights of the hunter. The photographers didn't want to kill me but they did kill something in me. They focus on you from far away and they steal something of your soul.' BB as a pre-technological primitive, fearful that the lens will possess her, like the devil? The idea is appealing. Which star has not, at one time or another, seen herself as a victim of the industry, a slave, exploited and oppressed, like the old horse in *Animal Farm*, yearning for liberation? 'Films annihilate and imprison you,' she complained in conversation with Françoise Sagan.

Nonetheless, Bardot would often fall for lensmen, tormentors and oppressors and gaolers or not. The case of Mike Sarne in *Two Weeks in September* was more than a scriptwriter's fantasy. In 1974, Laurent Vergez, aged twenty-nine, actor turned photographer, snapped her nude for *Playboy* (which ran the pictures as 'BB in her 40th-birthday suit') and was handsomely rewarded by becoming her lover; she traded him in come winter for Miroslav Brozek ('Mirko', also known mysteriously as 'Jean Blaise'), a Czech sculptor she met skiing in Méribel. If the lensman was a sadist, then she was a masochist.

But there is no facile antithesis between humans and animals. On the face of it, Brigitte Bardot had relinquished the role of BB. She was by now in her forty-first year and it was only with a growing sense of nostalgia that she could evoke youthful untroubled sexuality, without ambiguity or irony. Her sexual charisma, though still powerful, had become nuanced, more complex, ambivalent. But her dedication to animals was not a rejection of humans because her embrace of humans was never a rejection of the animal. She was always unswervingly committed to animal rights: or, more specifically, to the right to be an animal in the Nietzschean sense. 'What bestiality of idea,' Nietzsche wrote, 'if hindered from being a beast of action!' BB showed precisely how to be a beast, and how to treat people like beasts, coupling nightly with Carlos, Alfredo and Enrique, with Chava, Pepe, Sergio, and Ramón (*Viva Maria!*) before guilt and shame and self-repression and inhibition cut in. Her naturalist aesthetics led to the fantasy of a world without cameras, populated by instinct. She was a throwback to a lost age – one that perhaps never existed – of the noble savage, the untamed female, unclothed, unwarped by the weave of society, devoid of anguish and insincerity, premeditation and afterthought. While the rest of us were lost in the library of Babel and the Gaumont cinema, she alone inhabited nature.

Yet her attitude to animals was ambiguous. On location in Spain in the sixties she took pity on a poorly treated donkey and bought him from his cruel master. When her hotel refused to keep him in their garage she took the donkey up to her room for the night, naming him Romeo. Romeo was our role-model. Romeo lived the dream. In the eighties she gave shelter to another donkey on her farm. When its owner returned a month later he discovered she had had it castrated. That donkey for one would never be called Romeo again. He was an ex-stud.

I had moved into a house in Garrick Street near Preston Circus in Brighton which I shared with a social worker called Richard. That house was No. 7. Shortly afterwards, Angélique moved into No. 5.

She came from La Rochelle, the daughter of a farming family, and was as organic and wholesome as an unploughed field. Temping in a chemicals company, she had a strongly marked French accent, reminiscent of Bardot's in *Doctor At Sea*. The last place she'd lived in was Bournemouth and she pronounced this as *Boorn-a-moot*. Andy came out as *On-dee*. The entire English language was reconstructed in her mouth as something strange and extravagant and bubbling. When she spoke French she was merely charming, but when she broke into English she was devastating and laid men to waste for miles around. It was her voice I fell for, but it was complemented by a body that was compact and cherubic and thatched with tubular curls. I had two advantages over the mob that pursued her home: I spoke French and I lived next door. When she was tired of the effort of trying to speak English she could flop back on the couch of her maternal tongue with me.

I began by seeking her assistance with some English-to-French translations and soon we were mutually indispensable. Our friendly kisses became more than friendly, our embraces tighter, and one evening after struggling with a passage about Descartes from Bertrand Russell's *History of Western Philosophy*, we removed our clothing and lay down together, freely mixing French and English.

'Andy,' she pointed out, 'I am not protected.'

'That's OK,' I soothed her, 'I have a preservative.'

'Non, non, non! I do not like these things. They are not natural. I prefer to be natural, don't you?'

'Yes, of course, but . . .'

'Then I must go to the *médecin* and obtain the pills. I take them before, but I do not take them since a long time. I do not want to before. However now I do.'

She told me that I pleased her and I told her how much she

pleased me and the very next day she went to the doctor's and waved her box of pills at me like a testament of good faith and asked me to translate the instructions.

'No sex for a fortnight,' I translated, glumly.

There was a romantic aspect to this enforced abstinence. It was like she was being sent abroad for a year to test my fidelity, or I was being put away for a long stretch and she was promising to wait for me. We were both immensely heroic about it and stoical and loyal. It was true love at last and happiness was assured.

By an evil fluke of geography Hayley lived at No. 3, two doors down the street from me and one door beyond Angélique. I should have been contented with 5; 3 was a house too far.

Hayley was indisputably the most beautiful woman on campus. At thirty she seemed to belong to an older generation. She was tall and golden-haired, her body not a trifle less well moulded inside her golden skin. Everyone agreed she was the Ideal Woman, the objective universal in person. I suppose that all men wanted her, but she frightened many away who were intimidated and appalled by such perfection.

Like Bardot, Hayley had begun as a photographic model, first in her home town of San Francisco, then London, Tokyo, Paris. I still have a couple of portraits of her as she appeared in American *Vogue*, one wearing a shiny PVC mackintosh and the other a skimpy bikini, with her thumb in her mouth. In both she has a sheen like well-polished shoes. For all I know, she may even have featured on the cover of *Elle*. Like Bardot, she grew dissatisfied with her representations and yearned to be more than just a bundle of sense data in the eyes of magazine readers. Unlike Bardot she signed up for a degree at the School of Cultural and Communications Studies at Sussex. Vadim could without contradiction have appended another chapter to his memoirs: *Bardot, Deneuve, Fonda and Hayley*. Rod Stewart is probably kicking himself he never added her to his collection.

I had no fear of Hayley because I had no expectations. She was a Venus as remote as Pluto. I had once passed her on campus and passed her again about two minutes later, foolishly muttering, '*Déjà-vu!*' It was not only prissy and pretentious, but wrong as far as one of us was concerned. 'Really?' she said, aware of my existence for the first and last time, before proceeding along her path, as ineluctable as a comet's. She didn't even notice I was prissy and pretentious.

So it was with astonishment that, the afternoon I went to pay a visit to Helga, a musician I had met on my first day at Sussex and who lived at No. 3, I found Hayley opening the door to me, stark naked. I know I must have said something, because presently she was calling 'Helga, there's a nice young man to see you' up the stairs, in between crunching on a stick of celery. But my mouth was running on automatic: mentally my jaw was hanging wide open. To say 'she was a vision' would be misleading, because there was nothing in the least intangible about that downy triangular back, those spherical buttocks, those legs swinging tranquilly down the hallway in search of the sun that was moored over the back garden. Of Helga and my visit to her, beyond the fact that Hayley had moved in with her, I have no recollection whatsoever.

Anne, who owned No. 5 where Angélique lived, was the disciple of a guru called Cecil who came down from London and preached that, by practising his specific brand of meditation and signing over your soul to him, you could obtain whatever you wished for: you could literally make your dreams come true. Angélique, although she attended some of Anne's classes in a spirit of camaraderie, was immune to such utopianism; but it was during this period that, natural sceptic though I was, I started to think Cecil might have a point. I had better not dream too explicitly, otherwise there was a risk of my most embarrassing desires turning up on the doorstep where everyone could see them.

The next day Hayley swept past me, dashing up the street towards London Road station to catch the branch-line train to the campus at Falmer. She continued sweeping past me until one day, clad in t-shirt and panties, she called to me over two back garden fences, 'You don't happen to know anything about *Hamlet*, do you?' After writing most of an overly Oedipal exegesis of the prince for her, I began to be invited over for regular brainstorming sessions. Hayley would prepare salads of spinach and olive oil as I summarized Sartrean phenomenology for the purposes of background to a dissertation on the American black existential novel (Ralph Ellison's *Invisible Man*, I remember), or came up with arbitrary answers to such questions as, 'What do you think of Hegel, Marx and Husserl?'

These occasions were essentially businesslike. Hayley would always have important parties and the like to go to later and couldn't afford to spend all day on essays.

Perhaps it was just coincidence, but a crucial variable in our equation changed around the time I started going out with Angélique. I would almost say it changed at exactly the hour that Angélique was out filling her prescription. For approximately the first time, Hayley asked me what it was I was working on. I mentioned the poems of Baudelaire.

'But I just love the *Fleurs du mal*,' she drawled. She spoke as if she had been brought up on them. Perhaps she had.

'I'm just reading the Jakobson/Lévi-Strauss structural analysis of "Les Chats".'

'I would simply love to have you read me some sonnets.'

I proposed one of our usual rendezvous: a lunchtime, a tea-time, a coffee-break? But Hayley was not free until Friday evening at ten. Angélique asked me, as the clock struck ten and I bolted up from the sofa, why it was I was going to No. 3 at this late hour. I explained that it had to do with some work. I couldn't quite bring myself to say I was going to read poetry though, especially not Baudelaire. Hayley took a long while to answer and I was already turning away to go back to No. 5 when the door opened. She had clothes on this time, a nightgown, creamy and satiny, loosely knotted at the waist.

'Oooh, it's cold, isn't it?' she shivered. 'Come on up.' She went up the stairs and I followed.

When I got to her room, Hayley had already slid under the duvet. Her gown lay discarded on the floor. Her anglepoise, angled downwards, cast a wan pool of light over the cane table by the bedside.

'You came just in time,' she said. 'I'm so tired I was about to fall asleep. Now what are you going to read me?'

I proposed 'La Chevelure', in which the poet's mistress's hair is projected as a rippling golden fleece, a mane, a sensual map of the world, a ship, an ocean, Asia and Africa, sails and slaves, salt-air and palm trees, coconuts and musk and tar, rubies, pearls and sapphires, the heat of the day and the darkness of night: it is a

144

gourd of wine, a narcotic, an oasis, a nest of dreams. Hayley's hair, lustrous, shadowy, hung like ripe bananas from her pillow.

'Shall I sit on the floor?' I said, looking round for a non-existent chair.

'Sit on the end of the bed. You'll be comfortable there.'

I read 'La Chevelure'. Hayley sighed. 'That was so beautiful,' she said. 'To think he could see all that in a head of hair! What's next?'

I flicked through the pages of 'Spleen et idéal'. '"La cloche fêlée",' I said, 'how about that one?' This is the sonnet about the cracked and flawed bell that is the soul of the poet, and whose sound is that of a wounded soldier, abandoned beside a lake of blood, pinned beneath a pile of bodies, who struggles, stares and dies. I read it. Hayley sighed again and wriggled appreciatively beneath her duvet.

'You know, I won a prize for reading this at school. The Holmes French Poetry Reading Prize.'

'You deserve a prize,' Hayley said. 'Come to matron.' She half sat up and the duvet was around her waist and her long arms were around my neck and her unsupported breasts swelled against my chest and her lips pressed against my lips and she fell back against the pillows and I fell with her, cradled, mattressed, lullabied against that vast pillowy encompassing body.

'You know the poem you make me think of?' I said, coming up for air.

'Which one?'

'"La Géante".'

'Oh. Can you read it to me?'

I saw the giantess, I scaled the slopes of her enormous knees, I sauntered through the landscape of her lap, and when the fevered summers left her slumped across the countryside, I slept nonchalantly in the shadow of her breasts, like a peaceful hamlet at the foot of a mountain.

'Excuse me for a moment,' Hayley said, getting out of bed as unselfconsciously naked as Yvette Maudet in *En cas de malheur*. 'I'm just going to put in my coil.'

When she came back I was leafing through her copy of the *I Ching*.

'What are you doing?' she said.

'Seeking guidance on whether this is such a good idea,' I said.

'Silly boy,' she said, and took the book from my hand and flung it on the floor.

Over the next fortnight or so, I was subjected to the most rigorous education of my life. Into this short space Hayley packed enough theory and practice for a degree. She was a demanding tutor. If I deviated a jot from the stern tenets of Californian orthodoxy, if I slacked on my homework and failed to induce ecstasy, if I finished too soon or not soon enough, if I rushed or was too tired, then she was quick to correct my error and put my performance to the test all over again.

Obsessed, driven, drained, I had lost track of the passing of time and the imminence of Angélique's availability. Like a neglected wife whose birthday had been brutally forgotten, she had to call to remind me from work.

'The fifteen days have passed, and tonight I am free, *mon amour*.'

It wasn't until after ten that I knocked on her door and I took her out for a perfunctory drink then took her back to my house and took her clothes off. It was like walking into finals. I'd been a conscientious student, I'd done the revision all right, I was up till two the night before. I was confident enough of a first. Then my mind went blank, I had forgotten everything I'd learned, I waffled. There is a passage in the *Surrealist Seminars on Sex* (dating from the twenties) in which André Breton maintains that it is possible for a man to attain orgasm without ejaculation. Angélique would not have gone along with it. But she forgave almost everything. She was sympathetic: 'Are you tired, *mon chéri*? It will be better next time.'

And for a short while it was. But it seemed like every day, every night, I would be going past Angélique's door on the way to Hayley's. Even Angélique began to lose faith. 'Must you do so much work with Hayley?' She never really complained, but she must have suspected that the knowledge we were after was carnal. Angélique saw much more of her friend Nicole from Marseilles.

Hayley dumped me, sooner rather than later. Her work was done. She didn't need my help with her essays any more. She wasn't in, she didn't answer the phone. When I finally managed to pin her down in the back garden one sunny afternoon, she bluntly told me that she was looking for a long-term relationship, even marriage, and obviously I was too young for that and it would be better if we didn't see one another for a while.

Within twenty-four hours I had come to my senses. I was at Angélique's house, cursing myself for having deserted her and cursing Hayley and promising to reform. It was all true. No more lies. But Nicole was there too, watching me. I went out with Angélique once more, but Nicole was still there and still watching. Later Anne told me that Angélique and Nicole were having a full-blown lesbian love-affair. Now I was frozen out at No. 5 as well as No. 3. It remained only for me to take my leave of Richard at No. 7 and go into self-imposed exile.

Years later, I saw the two of them coming towards me, Angélique and Nicole, arm in arm, in some west coast port – Dieppe, I think. They might have seen me, but not for long because I fled in the opposite direction, diving down side streets and dark alleyways, on the run from responsibility.

# 25

## 1976–77

In the organization of the rhymes, the poet follows the
scheme: aBBa . . .

Jakobson and Lévi-Strauss, 'Baudelaire's "Les Chats"'

Had I been born French, I might have elected to join the Foreign
Legion. As it was, I had another avenue of escape: the Year
Abroad.

I wasn't the only one taking the easy way out. Where BB failed,
Raoul Lévy, the producer of *And God Created Woman*, succeeded.
Taking no chances, he shot himself in 1967. In assigning motive,
friends cited money troubles and the fallout from the latest of a
string of unhappy love-affairs. But there is an alternative theory of
causation. A few weeks before his death he had delivered his
valediction to cinema and specifically BB: 'The demystification of
the stars, due to too much publicity about their private lives, is
ruining the box office. There is no longer any mystery about
Bardot. The public knows too many intimate things about her life.
Bardot sells newspapers and magazines, but she does not sell
tickets.' Cinema, he seemed to imply, depends on mystery, enigma,
concealment, on precisely not revealing all; Bardot (he and Vadim
and Bardot, that is) had made the error of disclosing too much and
stripping away all the mythology and had therefore left film, like a
conjuror all out of white rabbits and bouquets, with nothing up its
sleeve. What is there left to do (except commit suicide) after the
totality of truth has been unveiled?

Sean French, in his 1994 book about Bardot, seems on the
brink himself as he empathizes with Lévy: 'Perhaps his despair
was actually a realization that the earthquake represented by
Bardot, the overtness of desire and its expression, would only
occur once, followed perhaps by a few trivial aftershocks. The

phenomenon could be explored and there might be meretricious attempts to repeat the original, but the revelation, such as it was, could only occur once.'

On one tumultuous day in Paris, as I put Garrick Street and Brighton behind me by watching two BB films back-to-back, I saw my entire life flash before me at twenty-four frames per second. And it was not just my life. Nor was it only BB's: I had the feeling I was bearing witness to some universal drama, the great wheel and its inescapable cycle of driving optimism and the disappointment of hopes, of light and darkness.

*Les Grandes Manoeuvres*, directed by René Clair, was made in the same year as *Doctor at Sea*, 1955. Bardot plays a photographer's daughter, Lucie, who falls for a soldier in 1914. Roy Armes in *French Cinema* describes her as 'light relief'. But she is more than an innocent among adults, a counterpoint to the highly formalized main players with their vertical sabres and tight breeches. While galloping cavalryman Armand de la Verne (Gérard Philippe with a Clark Gable moustache) accepts a wager to seduce a divorcée and milliner who looks like Meryl Streep, BB follows her uncluttered impulses in a straight line. Just as the imminent 'summer manoeuvres' will give way to the real thing as the First World War looms, so too Armand finds that he truly loves the woman he staked his money on – his first true love after an array of amorous deceptions and pretences. But he cannot convince her of his sincerity. 'I can never believe in you,' she protests, and even Armand finds it hard to believe in himself. In contrast, there is never any doubt about the guileless Lucie's emotions or intentions. Bardot escapes acculturation, seemingly immune to frivolity and tragedy alike.

*Don Juan ou Et si Don Juan était une femme*, the final collaboration between Bardot and Vadim in 1973, is as chaotic as the grammar of its title suggests. Even Bardot's protagonist blurts out 'It's too complicated!' when asked to explain what she is up to. She destroys a series of males and is herself in turn dragged down and – in the climactic scene, echoing the fate of Don Juan in hell – consumed by fire. The young, handsome priest (her current lover, Laurent Vergez) to whom she confesses her crimes, says (echoing Simone de Beauvoir) 'You'll never change.' But the terrible reality was that she had.

Watching was a painful, almost intolerable experience for me, like burning in hell. It was not just that Bardot has to go through some half-hearted lesbian moves with Twiggish Jane Birkin. Nor that she is supplemented and side-lined by Vadim's overblown imagery – cassocks and candlesticks, bows and arrows, spheres and mirrors, slabs of meat hanging from hooks, an orgy, the Eiffel Tower, a picture on the wall of naked women stretching into infinity. It was rather that, as I saw her struggling semi-suicidally in the flames, I felt as if everything I once held dear, all the dreams and desires of the sixties, was going up in smoke.

Like Monroe, BB had become a caricature of herself. By the seventies she was trapped, too old to be innocent, too innocent to emulate the more explicit, hardcore option of Linda Lovelace and *Deep Throat*, she was doomed to repeat herself but without conviction or passion. She refused even to see *Last Tango in Paris*.

Beyond the immediate disarray of my own emotions and ambitions, beyond Wendy and Hayley and Angélique, there was a broader, more pervasive disenchantment which affected me as much as Lévy. Brigitte Bardot had been a more powerful teacher than Mr Holmes, Mr Jones, Professor John Cruickshank and Roland and Françoise rolled up into one pedagogic bundle: if she had worn a gown and mortar board she couldn't have made the case more strongly that in nakedness was truth, or, more precisely, that *nakedness was truth*. The attainment of truth depended on the simple prerequisite of taking your clothes off. But although Bardot had seemed naked even if all she took off was her shoes, no one else in my experience, no matter how completely disrobed, was ever quite naked enough. That mind-shattering moment of revelation had still not yet occurred. At least Lévy had been present at the Big Bang. All I had was an accumulation of low-decibel squibs which would never add up to an explosion. The body of truth had become tangled, tousled, inextricable, impenetrable. Sex had been subsumed in semiotics.

I applied to teach in the deep south – Aix, Avignon, Marseilles; I was offered a job in Tours, the old centre of France in the Loire Valley, where the purest, most classical French was spoken, the tomb of Ronsard and Balzac. Teaching English to a handful of graduate students preparing their Agrégation whose English was already manifestly accomplished, and writing a desultory dissertation on 'Description in the French Novel', left me a lot of free time. I rented a room behind a green *porte cochère* on the rue de la Raille, attended classes on plainsong and took sporadic lessons in the flute. But what I vowed to master was the alexandrine.

I was no poet, more engineer or mechanic. I wasn't inventing a new model, only trying to figure out how the old one worked. You could hardly move in Tours for poets brooding over clutches of *vers libres*, whose every line was radically unlike every other and in which everything was permitted – uncounted syllables, non-rhymes, masculine and feminine endings shamelessly mixed as if in a Swedish sauna. I shied away from this chaos of novelty and fertility. The alexandrine, its twelve resounding syllables evenly divided by an immovable caesura into twin hemistiches, was enough for me, like a mouthful of thirty-two perfect white teeth to a dentist.

With Maurice Grammont's *Petit Traité de versification française* (1907) as my Bible, I rewrote my dissertation in alexandrines, mocking the baggy, random looseness of the novel. It was transformed from an accidental assemblage of ideas and observations into an irrefutable tractatus, from mere contingency into fearsome inevitability. Leaping from fiction to theatre, I transposed *Hamlet*'s anarchic iambic pentameters – almost prose, *mon dieu!* – into strict Racinian verse: masculine-masculine, feminine-feminine – and never the twain shall meet. But somehow Molière kept breaking in and the tragic solemnity of the soliloquies was warped by foolish comic asides. So it was that I turned for relief to the still tighter, mathematically rigorous form of the sonnet. Fourteen lines at twelve syllables a line, that made 168 syllables per poem, neither more nor less. Here lay certitude; everything else was a lottery. Stylistically, I was restricted to imitating Baudelaire, Nerval or Leconte de Lisle.

Where I went wrong was in boasting about my competence. 'I don't believe it,' retorted Sophie. Sophie de Wilde was *très mondaine* my friends had said, you must get to know her. She held a salon every Monday, at her apartment in the *vieille ville*. 'An Englishman writing French sonnets – impossible!'

She had spoken loudly and I was aware that everyone else in

the small room had tuned in to our conversation, as if spectators at a duel. 'There's no mystery,' I replied. 'It's just a question of obeying the rules.'

But my confidence only succeeded in enflaming her. 'And how long would it take you to write such a sonnet?'

'A few hours.'

'An afternoon, for example?'

'It's possible.'

'Then let it be *this* afternoon. Listen: there is a party tonight. The birthday of a girlfriend of mine. Why don't you come? And bring your sonnet with you.'

PBAP – a bring-your-own-poem party: that's the way Tours was. I was beginning to feel jittery about the idea, but it was too late to draw back. 'No problem. What subject would you like?'

'No cheating now. It mustn't be an old poem you've pulled out of your drawer. It must be written this very afternoon. For tonight.'

'"Sonnet on the Birthday of an Unknown Girl", would that suit you?'

'It would be perfect.'

'Her name?'

'Béatrice. Béatrice Beauregard.'

My anxiety evaporated: the name was a gift, itself a poem. All I had to do was stretch it to fit fourteen lines. I had already roughed out the argument and was ironing out a hitch in the rhyme scheme of the second quatrain when Georges called on me to play the game of tennis we had arranged. Georges Rivière was a footloose *flâneur* who did little but play tennis and chase women.

'Sorry, Georges,' I said. 'I have a sonnet to finish.'

'Chicken, eh?' he taunted. Georges had no understanding of art.

We compromised on one set and went to 7–6 before I broke him. I dashed back home from Georges's club and finished the sonnet, but had to rush the closing couplet, and arrived for the party with the ink barely dry on the squared paper.

The party was being held in one of the *salles privées* of *L'Univers*, an elegant domed hotel on the main street. It was owned, I discovered later, by Béatrice's parents, and she lived there. At the end of the evening, as Béatrice was unwrapping her presents, Sophie interrupted her. 'Your best present is still to come,' she said. 'A poem – dedicated to you.'

I was called upon to deliver my poem. The room fell respectfully silent. I declaimed 'Sonnet sur l'anniversaire d'une fille inconnue'. I remember I had to write 'Beauregard, Béatrice', partly in keeping with French protocol, partly to retain the feminine rhyme at the end of a perfect hemistich. Her name was exactly half an alexandrine. Loyal to *rimes embrassées* and, wherever possible, *riches*, fanatically permutating masculine and feminine lines, I pointed out that since the bearer of that heavenly name was unknown to me I had to rely on summoning up a purely imaginary Béatrice. But was she Dante's ideal figure of virtue who led him out of purgatory up to paradise? Or was she more of a Bébé, irresistible beacon of St Tropez (which I rhymed with *vous me dopez*: 'you drug me'). But I concluded – in that hasty final couplet – by complaining that ignorance was not bliss and that knowledge of the flesh-and-blood woman was bound to be superior to a fantasy of womanhood. It was way over the top, as was the applause with which it was greeted.

Just as well that the original is lost to posterity for, in this case, the fantasy is certainly superior to the real thing. The last rhyme depended, for example, on my mispronouncing *os* in the phrase *en chair et en os* ('in the flesh') to echo Bard*ot* rather than albatr*os* or Lesb*os*. The bit about the actual woman out-scoring any imaginary BB was just flattery, par for the course in this genre. For all I knew she could have been one of the Ugly Sisters. She and Sophie demanded to know how I could have written this formidable poem so quickly. The answer, I said, was that I had had for inspiration not one but two muses. They laughed politely.

As I stood before Sophie and Béatrice, the one dark the other fair, I couldn't help thinking of the sonnet by Ronsard in which he admires two women sitting next to one another, cousins, one as lovely as the dawn, the other like the sun. I remembered that while the more chaste and saintly one of the pair at least bestows a glance on the poet, the other – by whom the poet is obsessed – moodily and steadfastly ignores his existence. But, back at *L'Univers*, I suffered no such mixed reviews: the two were equally attentive, equally positive in their praise. I could do no wrong. All was well with the world.

'Sonnet on the Birthday of an Unknown Girl', that chrysalis of clichés, butterflied out into a regular meal ticket. The promise of it had already gained me one invitation to dinner; now the be-laurelled poem won me two more: Sophie insisted that I join her at her family home in the country the following day, Sunday, while Béatrice granted me a second audience in a week. I told Sophie I couldn't make it till the afternoon: I was playing tennis in the morning. But the following Saturday couldn't come soon enough.

Georges told me that Sophie was the only child of the Duc de Wilde who lived in a château at Azay-sur-Cher. She was an heiress and fabulously wealthy and well-known for her good works. '*Une femme et une fortune,*' he chuckled, covetously.

The gates to her family home stood some miles out of town; the château itself was the best part of a mile further on, at the end of a long avenue of plane trees, whose few leaves were golden brown, and directly overlooking the river Cher. The building itself – all crenellated parapets and cylindrical turrets – was encircled by a moat, fed by the river. Inside, the rooms were cavernous and ribbed with oak. The Duc was greying but strong-jawed and erect. He asked me to go hunting with him, I said I didn't go in for blood sports. 'Blood!' laughed Sophie, smoothing over the difference between us, 'we never catch anything anyway.'

I imagined that he imagined that I – an unscrupulous English gold-digger – was hot on the scent of his daughter and her dowry. In an excess of ethics, I was determined to prove him wrong. And I had other things on my mind.

As I kissed Sophie's cheeks goodnight, she brushed my lips with hers. The next day she came to visit me. She was just dropping in for coffee, she said. I didn't have any, I said. Dropping in for coffee was just a figure of speech, she explained: she didn't mind tea. We spoke of poetry and foreign countries and the plight of sterling. But all the while I was thinking of the work I had guiltily hidden away when she entered: my second 'Sonnet pour Béatrice'.

'Are you a fool?' Georges upbraided me. 'You cannot ignore Sophie like this: it is worse than a crime, it is a mistake. She is charming. She is rich. She is the richest girl in Tours.'

But I insisted on devoting that week to writing. Sophie invited me to accompany her to the Septième Art cinema nearby. But I had already seen the film. See it again! *Non, c'est impossible!* I was busy tearing up sonnets; nothing was good enough for Béatrice. Meeting her had ruined me. Only when my deadline was bearing down on me like an annihilating train did I wrench free of the ropes that held me down, leaving myself just enough time to polish and refine.

I arrived chez Béatrice with my verses sitting sweetly in my pocket. As I rang her buzzer, I was looking forward to an intimate tête-à-tête, crowned by bardic triumph and sexual conquest. Béatrice had scarcely kissed me before I babbled that I had brought her another poem. But she bade me put it away momentarily and led me through to a roomful of her friends. She sat next to a tall, broad-shouldered rugby-player named Christophe; I was several places removed from her.

'I nearly forgot,' Béatrice piped up towards the end of the meal. 'You have written me a poem. Another poem!'

'Read it for us,' said Christophe, 'I beg of you. Let us all hear.'

It wasn't what I had had in mind, but there was no choice. In my 'Second Sonnet to Béatrice', I took the writer's easy way out. When blocked, write about your block. At least it's something to write about. Logically enough, it was a sequel to the first sonnet. I promised to give up the illusions of poetry in favour of a still more poetic reality. I compared myself to a man dying of hunger and thirst who had just emerged from the desert and her to a good samaritan who had fed and watered me. I concluded by rhyming *désert* as richly as possible with *dessert* and wondering what the latter might consist of. I was happy enough with this soufflé after I had concocted it; but now, long before the fourteenth line, it had collapsed and the taste of it was bitter in my mouth.

In the brief pause between quatrains and tercets I glanced up and observed Béatrice gazing raptly at Christophe. It was Christophe, I knew, who was being fed and watered. I felt like a ventriloquist's dummy, Cyrano to his Christian, mouthing love poems for him. Leaving Béatrice's house, I shredded the ridiculous second sonnet and flung the ribbons into the darkly swirling Loire.

As I trailed wretchedly home, an old couple, who looked the worse for drink and gave off a damp smell, asked me the way to the hostel of the Sacred Sisters. It was certainly closed by now, I explained. Had there just been one of them, I might have been able to help, I said. '*On s'aime*,' they echoed one another: they could not be parted, not at any price. They ended up sleeping on the spare bed in my room. Both of them snored abominably, wracked by bronchitis. In the morning the Sacred Sisters refused to have them. I rang up Sophie. She found a hostel that would take them on the other side of town. I dropped them off, but they came straight back again, complaining that they would have been split up – '*On s'aime! On s'aime!*' they protested – and, moreover, would not be allowed to drink. Sophie and I eventually dumped them on the motorway out of town. Their parting words were '*On s'aime!*' For a while Sophie and I saw one another nearly every day. There was her salon, then dinner, a film, a concert. I had every opportunity to behave as I was already behaving in the Pilou-esque, hair-trigger imagination of the Duc de Wilde. Once she called round for coffee and came to sit on my bed. I recited a poem by, I think, Lamartine.

Georges tried to bring me to my senses. 'Listen, my friend,' he said, magnanimous after inflicting a crushing defeat. 'You are being offered a peach on a plate and you turn up your nose at it. You must be insane. Your Sophie, she is delightful; what makes Béatrice so wonderful?'

I found it hard to say. But faithful to some tortured notion of fidelity, I refused to betray Béatrice. Sophie's wealth only strengthened my resistance. And then, there was always an outside chance that Béatrice might chuck Christophe or (but this was straining credulity) vice-versa, and I had to be ready to step into the gap.

At the end of the academic year I returned to Sussex. Taking fright, I had re-transposed my dissertation out of alexandrines and back into prose. From then on I confined myself to essays and examinations. I was in the midst of finals when I received another invitation: the Duc de Wilde requesting the pleasure of my company on the occasion of the marriage of his daughter, Sophie, to Georges Rivière. Game, set and match to Georges. I sent a telegram – in French but without rhymes.

I never saw Béatrice again.

It was several summers later, when I was driving south through France, that it occurred to me to look up Sophie and Georges. I phoned and she invited me over. They greeted me at the door of their château. The Duke had died in a hunting accident. As Sophie introduced me to her two small children, she appeared to me far lovelier than I had remembered. A couple of lines of that old Ronsard poem about the two cousins floated back to me again:

*Te regardant assise auprès de ta cousine,*
*Belle comme une aurore, et toy comme un Soleil*

Sophie had been the dawn and Béatrice the sun. Now Béatrice had burned out, her unbearable, dizzying, stroke-inducing heat extinguished – and Sophie could emerge from the shadows. I was blinded by Béatrice: I had only ever seen her filtered through the Polaroids of poetry and the films of Bardot. Béatrice had taken over where Manina, Juliette, Babette and Yvette left off. Now the image had faded out and left Sophie, sitting at a table at one end of the tennis court Georges had built in their grounds on the banks of the Cher.

I watched her between points and it was as if I was seeing her for the first time. Georges took the opening set but I fought back in the second. We didn't push it to a third. Sophie embraced us both, with even-handed affection.

Over dinner, I asked about old friends. Béatrice? Married and living in Paris. Christophe was in Tahiti, at the University of the South Pacific. Sophie pressed me to remain, but I found some excuse to get on my way.

I regretted never writing any sonnets to her, to a known rather than an unknown girl. Now I was all out of sonnets. As I drove on south through the night, I understood that we had loved one another, but out of sync: first she loved me and I didn't notice, now I loved her and she would never know. Perhaps I had secretly loved her from the beginning, but was distracted from the truth; perhaps she still loved me and always would. But like the two hemistiches of an alexandrine, we were split forever by an unbridgeable caesura.

# 26

# Easter 1983

Il n'y a pas *La* femme, article défini pour désigner l'universel.

Jacques Lacan, 'Dieu et la jouissance de *La* Femme'

(There is no such thing as *The* woman, where the definite article stands for the universal.)

I was in Venice, steaming up the Gran Canal with an ophthalmologist, when I saw, as in a mirror, the image of my own obsession. I had found my doctor.

I was familiar with aversion therapy. Back in Brighton I moved into a house which I shared with a clinical psychologist named Alf. It was No. 3, Hayley's old house, which I had bought from Helga when she graduated. Alf introduced me to a patient of his who suffered from a rare form of compulsive behaviour: the exact opposite of a litter-bug, he was a man driven to pick up and pocket any stray piece of rubbish – crisp bag, Coke can, bus ticket, orange peel – blowing about the streets. Mike was not a man of exceptional public-spiritedness, intent on cleansing the environment, but a victim of a dark force which prevented him from getting from A to B without pursuing any and every scrap of detritus in-between. In a way, it was a form of perpetual deferral, a practical demonstration of Zeno's paradox, since – given the endless proliferation of litter – the poor devil could never make it to his intended destination. He was paralysed.

Alf analysed, counselled, drugged, all in vain, before resorting to what he called his ultimate deterrent: *enactment*. He joined the patient on one of his mazy, twisted expeditions through the knee-deep urban garbage. When Mike stopped and bent down, fatally drawn to a Rolo wrapper, Alf would stop and bend down to retrieve a cigarette butt; when Mike collected a Kentucky Fried Chicken box, Alf would make a trophy of a congealed condom. Each carried a sack which was soon overflowing with swag. Mike turned to Alf and said, 'Are you mad or something?' That was the breakthrough: henceforward, Mike could inspect his obsessive-compulsive disorder from the outside, like a detached observer, condemn it as irrational and cease of his own volition. He was cured. The cause of keeping Britain tidy had lost one of its most heroic campaigners.

Bruce, the vaporetto ophthalmologist, was in Venice for a conference on retinal detachment; I was en route from Rome to the Alps. We had been post-grads together at Cambridge. I had just had time to get off the train and on the boat for the Lido when Bruce fell prey to his equivalent of compulsive litter collection.

'Oh God!' he sighed. 'Isn't she beautiful?'

'Who?' I said, looking round for someone to measure up to his accolade.

'Her, of course, you berk.' He nodded towards a woman a few seats from where we were standing. She had wheaty-coloured hair, cut short, and a pale, consumptive complexion.

'Look at the bone structure.' It was just that that disturbed me. You couldn't *not* look at the bone structure. The bone structure was out there looking at you. She was all bone structure. High cheekbones, strong jawline, a sharp nose, the skull beneath the skin. Bruce jerked me forwards along the deck to get a better view, ostensibly of Venice, but actually of the exogenous architecture of this fellow passenger. As our gaze accidentally fell upon her, my queasiness intensified. She had an over-sculpted look, like a creature straight out of Modigliani. She was, in a word, thin. Her conversation with the woman next to her told us she was Canadian, a thin Canadian.

'She's a bit thin,' I said.

But Bruce wasn't listening any more. The vaporetto had pulled in and the two women stood up and strolled together down the aisle. Bruce tagged along behind them. I saw him follow them off the boat and into a hotel with a grand canopied entrance overlooking the canal. He spent the next couple of days lounging in the foyer, or stationed in the café outside, waiting for her to appear. He got as far as overhearing her name, but never once spoke to her. Only when she checked out did he relinquish his vigil, just in time to catch the plane home. 'She was too perfect,' he moaned. He saw almost nothing of Venice, his retina detached from the plenteous beauties of the city by the elliptical attraction of the thin woman.

The root of his obsessive-compulsive behaviour wasn't hard to dig up. Bruce had spent too much time in the Anatomy Room as a student. His image of Woman had been determined at an early age by a skeleton hanging from a hook in the ceiling – a body that nothing more could go wrong with. All women either approximated to or deviated from that impossible ideal.

Bruce was cured by his own excess: he had faced up to his calciferous fantasy and finally succeeded in getting it out of his system. When he got back to Cambridge he fell briefly in love with a broad-hipped big-breasted language student from Naples.

I had been in the thrall of a parallel aspiration after the ungraspable. I understood that Brigitte Bardot had been the alexandrine of my life, the rigid archetypal frame that I squeezed everyone else to fit into. She alone had the classical symmetry, the ratio of waist to hips, upper body to lower, the size of eyes and height of cheekbone, the double helix that constituted the underlying DNA of the cosmos. She had been around long enough to explode her own myth, but the fall-out spread like a virus, like stars, and clouded my perception of the world.

Venice had put my own obsession and repression on the couch. At last I could rationalize my irrational longings. I mentally deconstructed Bardot, disassembled this cinematic android into her hallucinatory parts. In the age of high Thatcherism, it was easy to understand Bardot as a mere commodity, a product designed to supply a demand, or to generate a demand she could satisfy and yet not satiate. The 1956 *Exhibitors' Campaign Book* of *And God Created Woman* (distributed by Miracle Films for the purpose of stimulating 'supplemental sales') sacrifices the star to a merchandizing perspective. Bardot is no longer a woman but a lurid collage of life-size shop-window cut-outs, a mosaic of 'tie-up stills' and 'go-getter gadgets' subordinate to a variety of markets: fashion (clothes on), beachwear (clothes off), bicycles (BB on the saddle), sports (a scene involving a dartboard), alcohol, pets, nylons, holidays, even newspapers. She metamorphoses into a 'full colour quad sizzler (3s)', a 'three colour double crown teaser (2s 6d)', or a 'special strip tease throwaway (£3 for 250)'. She is a dummy to hang your wares on. Even Raymond Pellegrin, in *The Light Across the Street* (*La Lumière d'en face*, 1955), playing the impotent and insanely jealous husband Georges, frozen as he peers out of a window, loaded and cocked rifle in hand, is described as 'still available for Sports Shop tie-up'. I – it was disgracefully clear to me – had been the hapless victim of an infamous product placement campaign.

Involuntary aversion therapy had saved me from myself, just as Alf had saved his patient Mike. There was just one snag with enactment, as Alf explained to me: it tended to provide only temporary relief. Aversion therapy worked all right, but the cure was not permanent and needed to be constantly reinforced. Mike was soon back hoovering the streets.

I went back to studying France and French literature. I wrote a book called *The Knowledge of Ignorance*, which purported to be an intellectual history of the relationship between the ideas of science, nescience and omniscience, starting with the Book of Genesis and ending with the *voyages extraordinaires* of Jules Verne. I suspect now that the only relationship it was about was the long-distance romance between BB and me. Like the wu-hsin ('no mind') of zen buddhism, like the *coincidentia oppositorum* of Nicholas of Cusa, Brigitte Bardot represented my own short-cut to *satori*. But 'knowledge of ignorance' encapsulated the full extent of my knowledge about Brigitte Bardot: I knew her and I did not know her. The more thoroughly I repressed her the more ruthlessly she erupted into my life, hydra-headed, invading my most sequestered inner sanctum. I set to work on a book about Napoleon.

Then one night I was having dinner with a visiting French film director. 'Napoleon,' he remarked, 'was the Brigitte Bardot of the nineteenth century – everyone was obsessed with him. Or maybe Brigitte Bardot is the *Napoléon de nos jours*.' Even Mike Sarne had acknowledged the analogy: when asked whether BB would regret giving up motherhood for stardom, he replied, 'What would you say to Napoleon on Elba? You climb into a boat, row over to the island and say, "Okay, Bonaparte, was it all worth it?" I mean, it's balls, isn't it?' I fled her into books and history, but there was no escape.

She was getting older. She was approaching fifty and I was over thirty. We were growing old together and her tastes had changed to accommodate me. 'I think back in horror at my ridiculous choice in men when I was much younger,' she told the *News of the World* in 1974. 'They would be the young fast ones – fast cars, restless souls, dancing-crazy and with a fund of infantile stories and jokes. Now I demand a man with a mind, a thinker with depth and understanding, someone who has lived, suffered a little like I have and bears the scars of emotional wounds.'

OK, I would have to ease up on my fund of infantile stories and jokes. But not content with giving up films, she put it about that she was retiring from the role of sexual adventurer as well. It was not even as if she was married, it was worse than that: her liaisons, those ecstatically ephemeral episodes were blossoming (if reports were true) from sonnet-size – from haikus! – into full-blown romances, novels, epics, soaps seemingly without end, lasting longer than her marriages ever had. She no longer discarded her lovers with the old casual extravagance, but hung on to them, like worn-out shoes and socks. The idea was unnerving.

I met my wife on the rebound. The affair could only last a week, I told her, or at most six. And then the weeks accumulated into months and the months into years. She was an Australian Yoko Ono with dark hair and almost no resemblance to Brigitte Bardot, although on our first date I did wonder if she might be Swedish. I was finally over BB.

Once upon a time, I made the mistake of ascribing everything good to BB; but there is a cruder mistake – blaming her for everything that is bad. Who done it? Brigitte Bardot. We feel instinctively it is her fault we got old. Once she was the soul of innocence, but by the post-Thatcherite nineties she has become the root of all evil: 'After Haight Ashbury, Charles Manson and Altamont,' laments Sean French, 'the dark side of the Love generation had been revealed.' It was as if Bardot herself had pulled the trigger. She had taken Rousseau and turned him around into the Marquis de Sade. 'By 1973 the sixties had already gone sour, it had all been done, sex on screen had become a cliché, sexual liberation was a familiar subject and people had long since moved on to consider the possible costs, whether "liberation" was necessarily the right word.' As if in a cycle of eternal recurrence, Bardot, like Napoleon, like General de Gaulle, had passed from liberator to tyrant, that from which we needed liberating.

The sexual revolution, touted as an absolute clarification of the truth, only compounded the confusion of genders. Bardot, the child-woman, the virgin-whore, the man-woman, contained a principle of ambiguity and uncertainty. 'It's because of Bardot that women do not exist,' L'Express commented bitterly in 1994. 'She killed them like Charlie Parker killed the saxophone.' Just as Madame Bovary was tricked into adultery by reading too much cheap romantic fiction, just as Molina in Kiss of the Spider Woman OD'd on MGM and saw himself as a vampish Holly-wood heroine, so we had all been brainwashed by movies into running after raptures that no actual experience could ever live up to. That was the theory. One way or another, everyone was under the thumb of a vast impersonal industry of delusion, shackled to an assembly line of production and consumption.

Now at last Bardot was being punished for being young and beautiful and free. Her face was inscribed with the infamy of decades. She had lain naked on the beach too long, a cigarette smoking dreamily between her fingers. From anticipating the sexual utopia of the future, she had passed irrevocably into recalling the sexual utopia of the past – before AIDS, transsexu-ality, Madonna and melanoma – without ever quite making contact with the present. She had been relegated to the status of a long flashback.

And that utopia itself had long since ceased to be utopian. Bardot's philosophical bedfellow was not Jean-Paul Sartre or Simone de Beauvoir, nor even Herbert Marcuse with his transcendent mix of Marx and Freud, but Charles Fourier, the sexual visionary of the turn of the nineteenth century.

In his doctrine of passionate attraction, Fourier saw himself as extending Newton to the organic universe. In the promised land of the phalanstery, when we are not ploughing the fields or writing operas, our butterfly passions will be exercised to the point of exhaustion. According to Fourier, no one should have to stick at anything – job, relationship, foreplay – for any longer than a maximum of two hours. Multiple affairs and public orgies will become the norm, and a sexual AA service will stand by in case of emergencies. Brigitte Bardot had been a one-woman phalanstery and we were queuing up to get in. Now all that seemed too much like hard labour. 'In the time of sexual liberation,' Jean Baudrillard writes in *Après l'Orgie*, 'the watch-word was the maximum of sexuality with the minimum of reproduction. Today, the dream of a clonic society seems rather the reverse: the maximum of reproduction with as little sex as possible.'

The two donkeys exhausted the options. In the sphere of sex, there are only two positions that really matter: *yes/no* or, electronically speaking, *on/off*. Bardot articulated both at different times, sometimes simultaneously.

In *War and Peace*, Tolstoy argues that Napoleon has been historically over-rated, romanticized out of all proportion. The point of the book is to deflate him. Napoleon was not the author of the battles he participated in; he did not create the French Empire. He was the tail that was wagged, not the dog itself. Just another soldier who happened to be alternately glamorized and demonized as the progenitor of good or of evil. The same case can be made for Brigitte Bardot: that she was the mercury in the thermometer, more effect than cause, the mirror of our ambitions and anxieties. But we had need of a first cause so we invented her as the temptress that seduced a generation. The strength of our invention was such that even she was another of its dupes. She seduced herself into thinking, for a while at least, that she was BB.

In his *Grand Erratum, source d'un nombre infini d'errata à noter dans l'histoire du dix-neuvième siècle*, Jean-Baptiste Pérès asserts that Napoleon Bonaparte never existed. He was nothing other than a poetic personification of the sun itself. He notes the resemblance of *Napoléon* and *Apollon*, decodes Bonaparte as light, and records that his career precisely emulates the course of the sun. His reign lasts exactly twelve years, like the hours of the day. He rose in the East (Egypt) and fell in the west (St Helena). Another writer suggests that *Bonaparte* ('good, i.e. bravest part –

of the French army') was simply an honorific term, a compliment, a military award conferred for valour in the field. No one individual could possibly have performed all the deeds that were attributed to him. Clearly Napoleon was an imaginary amalgam of heroism and grandeur and virtue and vice and murderousness and monstrosity.

Brigitte Bardot is another manifestation of atavistic sun-worship, a *reductio ad absurdum* of our palaeolithic superstition and desires. When I look at her films again, she never seems to me to be the same woman twice. Her features and form change radically from one film to the next: now fine and fragile, now outrageously blowsy and overblown. Even my five-year-old son, as I leafed through a book of her film posters, was moved to comment, 'She is always different,' before going back to his toys. She is not a single, indivisible being at all, but a jumble of heterogeneous percepts on which I have imposed an illusory unity. And she herself, we may hypothesize, felt the nothingness inside her and sought out others (I am one of them) to confirm her existence. Even in one and the same film, the images of her appear curiously unstable, discordant, indeterminate, as if imprecise doubles – stand-ins and lie-ins – had taken over at odd moments. Far from it being the case that there is no one else like her, it is as if there is no one who is not a little bit like her.

After her attempted suicide in 1960, the *pharmacien* in Menton who sold Bardot the bottle of barbiturates was asked why he had not recognized and questioned her: 'I serve a hundred Bardots every day,' was his answer. (Alternatively he didn't recognize her because he never saw her and she bought the pills in Paris.) BB is a composite concept, an Aristotelian derivative of the actual women we meet in the world, rather than their model and archetype. The ideal is unreal, a figment of our mythifying imagination. Vadim testifies to this suspicion when he says, 'Little by little there is nothing around her but emptiness. And she herself is becoming more and more empty.' But it was not just Roger Vadim who invested her vacancy with substance: it was Griffo, it was me.

Sometimes, at certain angles, under certain conditions, I look in the mirror, and I see Brigitte Bardot. Brigitte Bardot, *c'est moi*.

# 27

# August 1992–June 1994

Will I dig the same things that turned me on as a kid?
Will I look back and say I wish I hadn't done the things
that I did?

> The Beach Boys, 'When I Grow Up (To Be a Man)'

It was only when we got out of the battered Lada estate and walked along the sand that I realized that – unless you counted Dover or Boulogne, which I don't – it had taken us over twenty-four years to make it to the beach.

And even then it wasn't quite what we planned. The sand on the strip between Galway and Kinvara on the west coast of Ireland was black. Volcanic, I think. There was no one else for miles, not a soul, just the two of us and some frozen fish. A wind with teeth nipped at our exposed parts, which were few. The sea, beneath the iron-clad sky, echoed the colour of the sand.

General de Gaulle was dead; the Berlin Wall had crumbled; we had long since lost possession of the World Cup. And Griffo was bigger and heavier after a couple of decades in the building trade in Ireland, and none the worse for that. His hair was darker, the colour of his chocolate brown suit. A few years before he had almost drunk himself to death. Was it father-hood? Marriage? The loss of youth? No, it was his brother John. John had taken over a pub on the quay at Kinvara called 'The Auld Plaid Shawl' and Griffo was just doing what he could to encourage business from the other side of the bar. And then, to be honest, the Guinness itself was exceptionally creamy. But now he had given up the Guinness and stuck religiously to Ballygowan. John could look after himself. He had at least five kids – let them do the drinking! Griffo himself had acquired two girls and a boy, a dog named Tara, and a half-built house which he swore he would finish one day if it killed him.

He had no regrets, or if he had one regret it was that he had never run a newsagent's. He would have enjoyed the crack with customers. We skimmed stones across the water and tight-roped a jetty and fell to talking about Brigitte Bardot.

'What d'you think you'd do if she turned up on this beach right now?' Griffo said.

'Not likely, is it,' I said. 'It's not exactly St Tropez.'

'There's seals and dolphins down the coast. She could be coming here to see them.'

'And then she'd see us. Happy ending. Only about a quarter of a century too late.'

'Ah! It's never too late, ye pessimist. Look! Look out there!'

'What is it? BB swimming in to meet us?'

'Dolphins, look! You don't see them in this bay very often. They're here for the fish.'

And as I looked I saw first a group of sleek black fins slicing through the grey waters, and then an entire dolphin as it leapt up into the air, and then more dolphins, rocketing out of the waves and plummeting back down.

'I reckon she's still the most beautiful woman in the world,' Griffo said. 'So what if she is getting old? She was always the older woman. Nothing's changed. All right, she's a bit wrinkly – but Jaysus, you're a bit wrinkly yourself. And look at the competition. Madonna?'

'Cindy Crawford?'

'Sharon Stone? Pamela Anderson?'

'Hydroponic, grown in a vat.'

'God, I wish we had a few vats like that in Ireland,' Griffo said.

We drifted along the endless shoreline. 'Why do you think we failed to get to St Tropez?' I said.

'Failed? Who said we failed? We weren't even trying!'

'What about that night in the toilet?'

'That was a great night.'

'And all that bloody awful thumbing for lifts?'

'We were lucky.'

'Lucky! How the hell do you work that out?'

'We weren't ready. It was too soon. Just think about it, if we'd met her then, everything would have been different and we'd have missed out.'

'You mean, we *chose* not to make it?'

'We could have made it any time we wanted. We just didn't want it.'

I had always seen the story of our journey as a *voyage manqué*, an inglorious failure. But now Griffo was swinging me round to his more Panglossian stance: it wasn't that we had failed to attain BB, we chose not to, we had deliberately set out to make her unattainable. The theory made a kind of insane sense. It echoed Jack Palance in *Contempt*: Ulysses spun out his odyssey not because of the gods but because he secretly didn't want to see Penelope.

There was good reason not to when you looked at the evidence. John Lennon would often see her in his dreams, floating over his head like a halo or a flying saucer. In fact, she was taped to his ceiling. All his early paintings revolved around the same perfect impossible image. His first girlfriends tailored their looks to fit his fantasy and grew their hair long and full and dyed it blonde. He married a woman who resembled her from a distance. 'I want you, I want you, I want you,' he wrote, with Paul McCartney, in 1965, 'I'll get to you somehow.' Finally, in 1968, in his Maharishi period, he met her in a Mayfair hotel. He tried to compose her an instant song while she went out to dinner. He failed. In the same momentous year he married her precise antithesis and the Beatles split up. Looking back on their only unmediated encounter, he wrote: 'I was on acid and she was on her way out.' Later he was shot dead on a street in New York. His death seemed to confirm that to come face to face with the archetype was as doom-laden as opening up the tomb of Tutankhamun: there was a kind of curse upon her.

Bardot's insignificant others all got badly burned. Some never recovered. Most went mad. Bernard d'Ormale (her Mr Right-Wing, a National Front activist) was blasted out of Bardot's flat with tear-gas in punishment for booting the dogs out of the bedroom. Roger Vadim was condemned to repeat himself, forever making the same film and the same marriage, like a drunk telling the same joke over and over again. Jacques Charrier, like a monk, opted for a life of seclusion and painting.

Sachs dug himself into an extremely deep pit of deutchmarks. Had not Sarne himself admitted that BB had spoiled him for all time? 'I had more fun and excitement with Brigitte Bardot in the short time I knew her than with any other woman I have ever known.' In the aftermath of his liaison, he tried to make *The Road to St Tropez* and ended up with *Myra Breckinridge* on his hands instead. The last I heard of him (in 1994) he was making a low-budget update of *Romeo and Juliet*, called *The Punk and the Princess*, and proclaiming his return to orthodox Judaism. Essentially it was the mangy dog problem. Take a starving mongrel (as Bardot had once done on location in Spain), feed it a plateful of caviar and pâté de fois gras: and, logically, the old dog dies.

In other words: what did you do after BB? Whatever it was, it was sure to be an anti-climax. Our answer? Postpone BB for as long as possible.

'So we were saving her up?' I hypothesized.

'That's just the way it was. It would have been like giving Guinness to children. They don't really appreciate it. We were too young.'

'And now we're too old.'

'Fucked if we are! We're in our prime right now. Begod, she'd be lucky to have us.' He kicked a withered, semi-cemented boot at a rock. 'Let's go back. We'll do it properly this time. Take a motor.'

It was an itinerary I still travelled regularly in my mind. 'What about Vicky and Heather and the kids?'

'Bring 'em along. Bomb straight down the motorway. Ya-hoo! St Tropez, here we come!'

We planned to go in September, we had it all arranged, but Griffo had to finish off a big job. Then we rescheduled it for the following summer, and then the one after that.

In *Bardot: Two Lives*, Jeffrey Robinson devotes several pages to cataloguing those who made it to La Madrague. The stalkers began with long-distance swimmers, intrepid sailors, frogmen in rubber suits, helicopter pilots and numerous men claiming to be delivering flowers from the florist. Eventually, they came not single spies but in battalions: an armada of small craft anchored fifty feet off-shore; tour-boats with simultaneous translations in six languages; bus-loads of tourists parked outside her gates, gawping. Thieves, drunks, maniacs, underwear fetishists, men with Uzis, men with knives, public enemies on the run, they've all been inside La Madrague. Even Jeffrey Robinson. The place was a landmark, a national monument, as visited as Notre Dame. At the end of the eighteenth century, a Dr Joseph Monoyer, resident of St Tropez, noted that only young local boys swam there; now so many boys swam around her that Bardot herself had been forced to flee and take refuge, along with her animals, on a farm at Bazoches outside Paris. So many others had had the same idea, Griffo and I stand virtually alone in not knocking on BB's door. Maybe we were just shy. Maybe we wanted to be different.

It was early in 1994 that Jean-Marc Leblanc promised me my heart's desire. He was making a film about Cambridge for French television and wanted me to front it. I was only half-listening when he happened to mention the last programme he had made – a documentary about Brigitte Bardot. 'She has an aura,' Leblanc said. 'When you have that you never lose it. Believe me, you can't take your eyes off her. But she is unpopular in Paris.'

'Why is that?'

'She married a fascist – a friend of Le Pen.'

Of course she had married a fascist. Were not all men, one way or another, fascists? And was it not her destiny to marry all men? Therefore her marriage was an exemplary one, an abbreviation, a synopsis. The one stood for the many. Again, like all marriages, there was something impermanent and ambiguous about it and Bardot's early exclusives about secret weddings and long-term love were quickly overtyped with equivocation and back-pedalling. The husband, as usual, would end up on the cutting-room floor. Even now I am unsure as to whether she is married or not and, for that matter, whether she ever was.

'I've always wanted to meet her,' I said.

'That is easy,' he said. 'She liked my film. She liked me. We are friends.'

A few weeks later my phone rang and there was a French voice, female, on the other end of the line asking if this was M. Andy Martin. My pulse doubled, then trebled. The back of my neck froze. My brain went into spasm. At last, after standing me up for a lifetime, Brigitte was ringing to ask me for a date. 'C'est moi,' I confirmed.

'*Brigitte voudrait savoir . . .*' It wasn't Bardot after all: it was Leblanc's PA. Brigitte was jumpy about journalists. She wanted to know what I wanted to know. Everything, I said, more or less. Brigitte wanted to talk about animals. Fine, I said, I'm a vegetarian. Could I send a letter listing the questions I wanted to put? And they would let me know. She gave me a Paris address.

I didn't want to talk about animals. But my first letter was polite, respectful, diplomatic, discreet. *The Times* had asked me to interview her on the eve of her sixtieth birthday. I had been interested in her professionally for some time. My project was three-fold: 1. put the British public *au courant* of her activity in regard to animal welfare matters; 2. recall her earlier career; 3. situate her attitude towards the images and myths she had engendered.

I was already pushing my luck. I could tell from the PA that Bardot would rather not talk about BB. And yet why was I speaking to her if not for BB?

My second letter went right over the edge.

1. What did you see in Mike Sarne?
2. Was there anything between you and Sean Connery?
3. Why did you (a) marry (b) divorce Gunther Sachs?
4. Where were you and what were you doing in July 1968 and what were your feelings towards fifteen-year-olds?

    I never heard back from Bardot.

SAGAN: What effect does it have on you when you receive mail saying, 'I desire you'? Is it funny, depressing, or exciting?
BARDOT: Nothing, nothing at all. Those letters are completely beyond me. I look at them and throw them away.

*Observer Magazine*, 20.6.76

I had blown it. It is obvious now I had wanted to blow it.

Since then people have been competing to introduce us. A marine photographer wanted to shoot us swimming like fish and mobbed by dolphins. I got a letter from F. W. L. 'Fin' Martin, a retired Air Force engineer from Weston-super-Mare, who had made a collection of old ten-shilling notes autographed by kings and presidents and billionaires and heart-transplant pioneers and the first man on the moon and the last hangman in Britain and celebrities from Elvis to Nureyev, from Shirley Temple to Mae West. 'If they haven't made it to the top, I don't want them,' said Fin. He was asking me to fix him up with a lecture slot, but the thing that caught my eye was a photocopy he'd attached of a ten-shilling note bearing the signature of Brigitte Bardot. 'Brigitte Bardot' (the two names run together into one, the 'R' upper-case as well as the 'B') appears directly under the picture of the Queen, over-writing the signature of the Chief Cashier of the Bank of England. Above the Queen and precisely centred is a photograph of BB in her prime, with smile and pout and hair blowing in the breeze; the Queen is wearing a prim, thin-lipped, disapproving look. The other words on the note are: 'I promise to pay the Bearer on Demand the sum of Ten shillings.'

I once found a ten-shilling note in the alleyway at the end of Highfield Road when I was twelve, and it paid for an outing to the pictures for Griffo and me, and for choc-ices in the interval and the bus fare there and back. And we still had change at the end of it. The teaser-trailers that we were brought up on seemed to say to us that BB too promised to pay the bearer on demand her face-value. We fully expected her to yield her equivalent in solid gold. But the ten-shilling note ceased to be legal tender around the time Griffo and I set out on our pilgrimage and became a collector's item instead. Harold Wilson ushered in devaluation with the glib reassurance that 'the pound in your pocket' would still be worth a pound. But he said nothing about ten-shilling notes.

The realization came to me that Fin Martin had had more intimate contact with Brigitte Bardot than I had ever had.

'Don't go!' people said to me, when I was contemplating going over to see her. 'She's such a sad figure now. Old and ugly, when she was once so beautiful.' In his closing paragraph Sean French says much the same: 'Sex, the sunlight, and Saint-Tropez have decayed in their different ways and Bardot has become an old woman. But Juliette, the heroine of *And God Created Woman*, has been proved right, preserved on celluloid in all her youth, defying propriety and time with nothing but her pout and insolent beauty.' French is happy to revisit the star, but has no desire to visit the woman.

But it wasn't that at all. It wasn't that she was too old for me. I was more anxious that I would be too old for her. She might be sixty, but I was forty and not even cryogenically frozen on film. 'Our feelings may have changed completely from what they were in the 1950s,' writes French. Mine haven't changed since I first laid eyes on BB in Camber Sands. I find that I have remained faithful for over thirty years to the woman who made a philosophy out of infidelity.

There was another good reason for not going to see her. It was the reason that Simone de Beauvoir articulated around the same time I was falling in love in that amusement arcade. 'If we wish to understand what BB represents, it is useless to make the acquaintance of the young woman named Brigitte Bardot.' This is not a biography. Call it a mythography. Call it a love-letter. I feared that making the acquaintance of the old woman named Brigitte Bardot would get in the way of writing this book. If I were to zoom in too close to the real then I might lose all sense of the unreal, the ideal. Privileged inside information might end up destroying the myth, destroying me.

I am fond of Freud's argument (which even Marcuse in the end tolerates) in *Civilization and its Discontents* to the effect that sublimation is the bedrock of culture, art, music, literature. Or, as Griffo once put it: footballers are not allowed to have it away on a Friday night so they're still hungry for the big match. But there is no big match. Everything is either pre-match training or post-match analysis and commentary. Sex itself always eludes us. Sex, like Brigitte Bardot, is unattainable, a spectacular sign with a fugitive referent. Sex is an illusion about which we have forgotten that it is an illusion.

There was always the risk of a passionate illusion with Brigitte Bardot. But there was the certainty, if I went to interview her in St Tropez, of fulfilling at least the dream of meeting her. And that would be one dream less to dream. From Jean-Paul Sartre I had long since learned that satisfaction is the death of desire. Premature ejaculation summed up the limits of my original intentions with respect to BB; now at last I was more in tune with Serge Gainsbourg's 'Je me retiens.' I had wanted her fully, intensely, obscenely visible; now I preferred for her to remain the image she has always been from the very beginning. I, who once craved her naked truth, find myself satiated by secrecy.

We had been possessed at the climax of the sixties by the sensation that we were living, or at least intending to live, something radically novel and also definitive in the field of sexual relations, the beginning and the end. Humanity had at last achieved maturity or modernity or freedom or innocence, fulfilled its potential, maximized its potency. But in sex as in art there is no such thing as progress. In the *Symposium*, Socrates is instructed in the lore of love by Diotima, who has a vision of *to kalon*, the beautiful:

> First of all, it is ever-existent and neither comes to be nor perishes, neither waxes nor wanes; next, it is not beautiful in part and in part ugly, nor is it such at such a time and other at another, nor in one respect beautiful and in another ugly, nor so affected by position as to seem beautiful to some and ugly to others. Nor again will our initiate find the beautiful presented to him in the guise of a face or of hands or any other portion of the body, nor as a particular description or piece of knowledge, nor as existing somewhere in another substance, such as an animal or the earth or sky or any other thing; but existing ever in singularity of form independent by itself, while all the multitude of beautiful things partake of it in such wise that, though all of them are coming to be and perishing, it grows neither greater nor less, and is affected by nothing. (210E–211B)

BB was nothing other than the beautiful. Brigitte Bardot could only coincide with the myth, if she ever did, for a moment. Aged fifteen, Griffo and I had counted on being present for that moment, but we missed it and no amount of reminiscing will bring it back.

There are times when ignorance is a higher form of knowledge.

In the *Cambridge University Guide to Expertise* if you look up 'Black Holes', you'll find the name Stephen Hawking against it. I am under 'Brigitte Bardot'.

# 28

# 1995

In the chilly hours and minutes of uncertainty
I want to be
in the warm hold of your loving mind,
to feel you all around me and to take your hand
along the sand,
ah, but I may as well try and catch the wind
Donovan, 'Catch the Wind'

In February 1995 BB came back to England. I've often fantasized about her coming to my funeral – after I've jumped off the Eiffel Tower or blasted my brains out or taken an overdose, careful to leave a poignant, tear-jerking note – and sobbing as they lower the coffin into the earth or the ovens swallow me up and regurgitate a small urnful of dust. Now here she was in Coventry for someone else's funeral: Jill Phipps, 'the Joan of Arc of animal rights' as Bardot called her, a martyr to the veal trade, crushed under the hooves of a hundred calves, involuntary passengers aboard a juggernaut bound for the Continent.

Her appearance in Coventry – splashed across front pages and beamed through television screens – was as widely publicized as if it had been the Second Coming. And in a way it was. She came first, more than twenty-five years before, to Chiswick, to bowl over Mike Sarne, and now to Coventry to bury Jill Phipps. Maybe she too has fantasized about her own funeral ('in the final analysis,' she once told Françoise Sagan, 'death is not atrocious') and, at Coventry Cathedral, imagined that she was not burying just a comrade from across the Channel but laying to rest once more, for the last time, the myth of BB. But you cannot exterminate a myth, you only resuscitate and revive it in the very effort of killing it.

'She's not what she once was, is she?' said people who might otherwise never have remembered BB at all.

Friends stopped me on the street, at the nursery, at the baker's, at the Faculty, and said, 'Hey, Andy, why aren't you in Coventry? You haven't blown it again, have you?'

'Daddy, who is Brigitte Bardot?' asked my son.

Call it pride, but I wasn't going to be one of the crowd, straining to peer over the heads of a hundred anonymous on-lookers and fans. I didn't want to see her out the far end of a periscope. If only I'd had a longer lens on my Canon, I might have pulled off a Sarne yet and been yanked out of the mass and gone underground for a week. But she didn't call and I didn't go. She had already sent me to Coventry once and I was damned if I was going there of my own accord.

There is a novel by Arthur C. Clarke where an alien starship appears on the edge of the solar system heading towards earth. Scientists, christening the craft *Rama*, puzzle over its purpose and meaning: is it good or evil? Does it come to save us or annihilate us? In the end, it swerves away, bouncing off our atmosphere and setting a course for an unknown destination. The vessel is just passing through, indifferent to – perhaps ignorant of – our very existence.

And so it is with BB. BB is my Rama. The close encounter I anticipated for so long never happened. Our orbits briefly intersected, but she slipped right by me, angling off at a tangent into outer space, inexorable, irretrievable, impenetrable.

BB, I love you, me neither.

# Acknowledgements

I am indebted to Steve Griffin, not only for saying what he said the first time round, but for helping me to recall some of it much later.

Brigid Callaghan and Rose Wild of *The Times* were unwittingly instrumental in provoking this book when they packed me off on a 'Passport to France'. And Ilona Roth of the Open University pushed it along with her conversation on the Objective Universal and other things.

Thanks to Gertrude Erbach in *The Times* library and Shirley Griffiths in Bristol for giving me access to their archives. To the BFI for letting me see some of the lost treasures of the Bardot canon. To Fin Martin for his ten-shilling notes. And to Sophie de Wilde for offering to introduce me to BB finally.

I am grateful to Gilbert Adair for correcting my French and my English, to Ruth Rendell for reading yet another book among all the Bookers, and to my agent Sara Menguc and my editor at Faber Walter Donohue for all the constructive and deconstructive criticism.

But my most heartfelt gratitude goes to Heather – Beauvoir and Bardot in one – who always has and deserves to have the last word.

# Notes

I have drawn tentatively on the biographies of Bardot cited in the bibliography. More specific sources are given below with reference to the relevant page. If we were to take all these at face value Bardot would have said, at one time or another, everything it is possible to say and its exact opposite. Place of publication is given only if not either London or Paris.

4  Barry Norman, *Daily Mail*, 3 September 1966.
5  Carolyne Palmer, *Daily Express*, 20 October 1966.
7  *Sunday Times*, 11 September 1966.
17  Herbert Lottman, *Albert Camus*, 1978, p. 52. I have allowed myself a slight abbreviation of the original French.
20  Edgar Morin, *Les Stars*, p. 61.
21  Hortense Powdermaker, *Hollywood the Dream Factory: An Anthropologist Looks at the Movie-Makers*, Boston, 1950, p. 248.
22  *Daily Express*, 20 October 1966.
23  Marguerite Duras, *Sun*, 19 September 1964.
23  Father Marie-Dominique Bouyer, quoted in the *Daily Mail*, 10 August 1966.
26  Michel Butor, 'Jules Verne et les points suprêmes', *Répertoire*, 1960.
26  In the original *L'Etre et le néant*, 1943, p. 44.
27  Oxford Institute of Experimental Psychology in *Daily Mail*, 2 September 1966.
29  Plato: for example, the *Greater Hippias*.
29  Aristotle's *Metaphysics*. The best refutation of Plato is provided by Plato himself in the *Parmenides*.
35  Monsignor James T. Lyng is in Glenys Roberts, *Bardot*, p. 133.
35  Mario Vargas Llosa, *The Real Life of Alejandro Mayta*, New York, 1989, p. 18.
35  Donald Zec, *Daily Mirror*, 4 September 1956.
36  The American commentator was Walter Winchell.
37  Bardot writes in the *Daily Express*, 11 November 1975.
38  Vadim's *Memoirs of the Devil*.

46 The voyeur theory about Vadim, most recently espoused by Sean French in *Bardot*, is given plenty of credence by Vadim himself.

47 *The Times*, 31 January 1963.

48 Roberts, p. 208. Jeffrey Robinson in *Bardot: Two Lives* is particularly useful on Charrier. Also Peter Haining, *The Legend of Brigitte Bardot*.

53 Roberts, p. 210.

58 Simone de Beauvoir's essay, 'Brigitte Bardot and the Lolita Syndrome', appeared in 1960 as a slim book, published by André Deutsch.

61 Deirdre Bair, *Simone de Beauvoir: A Biography*, p. 379.

61 Charles Fourier, *Le nouveau monde amoureux*.

62 The sex-change theory is recorded in Roberts, p. 239.

66 Borges's 'The God's Script' is in *Labyrinths*.

84 From the last chapter of *L'Education sentimentale*.

85 Barbicane, chapter 7, 'Un moment d'ivresse', *Autour de la lune*, pp. 109–110, Livre de poche.

86 Herbert Marcuse, *Eros and Civilization*, 1956.

94 This story really exists somewhere.

100 The Hoover story is reported in Robinson, p. 150.

101 I particularly cherish the revolutionary slogan reported in René Viénet, *Enragés et situationnistes*, 1968, p. 301: 'Le football aux footballeurs!'

101 I have borrowed the definition of literature from Borges, 'The Wall and the Books', *Labyrinths*.

102 '35 avenue de la Bourdonnais' is the birthplace given by most biographers.

104 Bardot's first apparent suicide attempt dates back to her seventeenth year. Roberts, p. 74.

108–9 I have condensed the script as published by Faber and Faber.

111 Roland is probably thinking of Barthes's *Mythologies*, 1957. Apparently Barthes was commissioned to write a *mythologie* on Bardot, but it was never written.

118–9 The dialogue is borrowed, with only very small revisions, from the opening scene of *Le Mépris*.

125 Marcel Proust, *Du côté de chez Swann*, p. 372 in the Pléiade edition. The translation is C. K. Scott-Moncrieff's.

127 *De la grammatologie*, 1967, p. 429.

127–8 *Memoirs of the Devil*, p. 89.

133 The earlier Duras article is collected in *Outside: papiers d'un jour*, 1984, pp. 246–9. The later is in the *Sun*, 19 September 1964.

132 The *Daily Herald* quote is given by Peter Evans, *Bardot: Eternal Sex Goddess*, p. 68.

133 Sartre's waiter is in *L'Etre et le néant*, p. 95.

135 Roberts, p. 172, gives the text of the real/invented suicide-note. Jeffrey Robinson is among the sceptics on this point. For broader scepticism about the 'suicide', see Leslie Mallory, *News Chronicle*, 11 October 1960, 'L'Affaire Bardot'.

137 Barthes, *Fragments d'un discours amoureux*, 1977, p. 41. The translation is, with one or two minor modifications, that of Richard Howard.

138 A version of the 1974 conversation with Françoise Sagan was published in English in the *Observer Magazine*, 20 June 1976.

140 A. R. Orage, *Nietzsche in Outline and Aphorism*, 1907, p. 55.

140–1 The second donkey story is covered fully in Robinson.

146 *Recherches sur la sexualité*, translated by Malcolm Imrie as *Investigating Sex: Surrealist Discussions 1928–1932*, edited by José Pierre, 1992.

148 The essay is in Roman Jakobson, *Huit questions de poétique*, 1977, and *Language in Literature*, 1987.

148 For Lévy etc., see French, p. 140.

158 *Le Séminaire: livre xx. Encore*, p. 68. Translation in *Feminine Sexuality: Jacques Lacan and the Ecole Freudienne*, edited by Juliet Mitchell and Jacqueline Rose, 1988.

161 The director in question is Alain Cavalier.

161–2 Sarne in Evans, p. 110.

162 *News of the World*, 11 August 1974.

162–3 French, p. 158.

164 Baudrillard, *La Transparence du mal*, 1990.

165 Vadim, *Sunday Telegraph*, 25 September 1977.

168 John Lennon, *Skywriting By Word of Mouth*, 1986. Plus Ray Coleman, *Lennon: The Definitive Biography*, 1995.

169 Sarne in Evans, p. 108.

169 Robinson, pp. 5–10.

170 Monoyer is cited in Alain Corbin, *Le Territoire du vide: L'Occident et le désir du rivage (1750–1840)*, 1988, p. 101.

175 Conversation with Sagan, *Observer Magazine*, 20 June 1976.

176 Arthur C. Clarke, *Rendezvous with Rama*, 1973.

# Bibliography

I have cited only those texts strictly relevant to Bardot. All other works quoted or referred to are given in the Notes.

Simone de Beauvoir, *Brigitte Bardot and the Lolita Syndrome*, 1960
  *Cahiers du cinéma*, May 1957, 'Du petit ABBCédaire'
George Carpozi Jr, *The Brigitte Bardot Story*, undated
Tony Crawley, *Bébé: The Films of Brigitte Bardot*, 1975
Peter Evans, *Bardot: Eternal Sex Goddess*, 1972
Sean French, *Bardot*, 1994
Peter Haining, *The Legend of BB*, 1983
Alberto Moravia, *A Ghost at Noon* (the text *Le Mépris* is based on), 1959
Edgar Morin, *Les Stars*, 1972
Glenys Roberts, *Bardot: A Personal Biography*, 1984
Jeffrey Robinson, *Bardot: Two Lives*, 1994
Roger Vadim, *Bardot, Deneuve, Fonda*, 1986
—, *Memoirs of the Devil*, 1976

# Filmography

The fullest and most reliable filmography can be found in Sean French. My own flagrantly incomplete list simply reflects the films that, one way or another, mean something to me or that I have some affection for.

*Le Trou normand* (Crazy for Love; Ti Ta To), 1952.

*Manina, la fille sans voiles* (The Girl in the Bikini; The Lighthouse Keeper's Daughter), 1952

*Act of Love*, 1953, with Kirk Douglas

*Tradita* (Haine, amour et trahison; Night of Love), 1954

*Helen of Troy*, 1954

*Doctor at Sea*, 1955, with Dirk Bogarde

*Futures vedettes* (Sweet Sixteen), 1955, written by Roger Vadim and Marc Allégret; directed by Allégret

*Les Grandes Manoeuvres* (Summer Manoeuvres), 1955, written by René Clair and others, directed by René Clair

*La Lumière d'en face* (The Light Across the Street), 1955

*Mio figlio Nerone* (Nero's Mistress; Nero's Weekend), 1956

*En effeuillant la marguerite* (Please Mr Balzac), 1956

*Et Dieu créa la femme* (And God Created Woman), 1956, written by Roger Vadim and Raoul Lévy; directed by Vadim

*En cas de malheur* (Love is My Profession), 1957, with Jean Gabin

*Babette s'en va-t-en guerre* (Babette Goes to War), 1959, with Jacques Charrier

*La Vérité* (The Truth), 1960, directed by Henri-Georges Clouzot, with Sami Frey

*La Bride sur le cou* (Please Not Now), 1961, 'artistic direction' by Vadim

*La Vie privée* (A Very Private Affair), 1961, written by Louis Malle and Jean-Paul Rappeneau, directed by Louis Malle

*Le Mépris* (Contempt), 1963, directed by Jean-Luc Godard, with Jack Palance and Michel Piccoli

*Une ravissante idiote* (A Ravishing Idiot), 1963, with Anthony Perkins

*Viva Maria!*, 1965, written by Louis Malle and Jean-Claude Carrière, directed by Louis Malle

*Masculin-féminin* (Masculine-Feminine), 1965, written and directed by Jean-Luc Godard.

*A Coeur joie* (Two Weeks in September), 1967, directed by Serge Bourguignon, with Mike Sarne

*Shalako*, 1968, with Sean Connery

*Don Juan ou Et si Don Juan était une femme* (Don Juan or If Don Juan Were a Woman), 1973, written and directed by Vadim, with Jane Birkin